A Little Bite of Happiness

To my beautiful daughter who is kind enough to let me share our favourite recipes with the world

Published in 2016 by V.P Colombo

Text and illustrations copyright © V.P Colombo 2016

The moral right of the author has been asserted.

All rights reserved. No part of this book may be reproduced or transmitted by any persons or entity, including internet search engines or retailers, in any form or by any means, electronic or mechanical, including photocopying (except under the statutory exceptions provisions of the Australian Copyright Act 1968), recording, scanning or by any information storage and retrieval systems without the prior written permission of the author.

National Library of Australia Cataloguing-in-Publication entry has been applied for.

ISBN 978-0-9945552-7-4 (Ingram Spark)
ISBN 978-0-9945552-8-1 (Traditional Print)

Custom book production by Captain Honey
Cover and internal design by Natalie Winter
www.captainhoney.com.au

5 4 3 2 1   16 17 18 19 20

A Little Bite of Happiness
V.P Colombo

42 short stories
24 French recipes

Captain Honey
WWW.CAPTAINHONEY.COM.AU

Contents

The First Bite 1
Genesis 3
Ritual 6
Alchemist of Flavours 7
Creation 10

REMINISCENCE

Pain Perdu (Stale Bread) 15
Pain Perdu – Recipe 17

Clafoutis 19
Clafoutis aux Cerises – Recipe 20

Tarte aux Pommes 21
Full Butter Puff Pastry – Recipe 25
Salted Butter Caramel – Recipe 26

Grandma's Remedy 28
Grog – Recipe 30

The Maid 31
Madeleines – Recipe 35

Time Machine 36

He Was Like Chocolate 38

WHIMSICAL

The Kitchen Goddess 43

The Maya Vestal 46

Origination by the Moon 49
Mistress of Spices Macarons – Recipe 51

Bacchanalia 55

Opera 58

APHRODISIA

The Fallen Angel 62

The Lover 65
For One Mug of Solitary Pleasure – Recipe 67

Romance 69
Lover's Chocolate Mousse – Recipe 71

Paris: A Romantic Fantasy 72
Crêpes – Recipe 75

Tango Argentino 76

Chantilly Cream 77
Crème Chantilly – Recipe 79

A Man Cooking For You 80

Desire 83

Lady Velvet 85

Jealousy 86

Sweet Poison 89

EXOTICISM

Bosphorus 93

Garden of Roses 94
Kandahar Cake – Recipe 97

Josephine Baker 98
Josephine Baker Cake – Recipe 101

Tropical Beauty 102

Caribbean King 104
Vanilla Rum – Recipe 105
Carribbean Rice Pudding – Recipe 105

Seraglio 106

OBLIVION

Guilt 113

She Devil 114

The Devil's Chicken 117

Find What You Love... 121
Blissful Lemon Tarts – Recipe 124

The Heaven's Cook 126

The Painting 131
Apple-Pear Puree – Recipe 135

INFANCY

Berries 139

Sweet Berries 143

Christmas Shenanigans 145
Petits Sablés de Noël – Recipe 147

Cheeky Little Girl 148
Chocolate Truffles – Recipe 151

Clémence's Cake 152
Chocolate Cake – Recipe 154

The Bet 155

Friendship 157

PUNGENCY

I Am an Addict 163
Risotto al Gorgonzola e Riesling – Recipe 165

Pastoral Getaway 167
Raclette – Recipe 171

About the Author 173

The First Bite

Taking the first bite is a very intimate moment. Like a slow dance, it is just you and your senses, detached from your surroundings.

Seeing its shape, roundness, colours, shades…you are languishing for this promise of sensations, inventing a beautiful story of how it is going to feel, letting your imagination flow like the origination of a romance.

The first nibble, your eyes closed, allowing all the flavours to play around your palate, exciting your taste buds, aromas flowing through your nose. That is when you capture the entity of this divine morsel of food, its wholeness, its deliciousness.

This discovery of a new dimension, a genuine intimacy between you and the saveurs, the textures, might bring you back to childhood memories — a place, a special day, a cuddle, a kiss, a comforting feeling in your granny's kitchen — or to travel memories — the warmth of the sun, the salt of the ocean, the incredible colours and spices of a foreign country — or even to the land of impossible dreams, fantasising about a place yet to be found.

But one thing is sure: this is your time, yours only…and you just had a little bite of happiness.

Close your eyes and shut the door to the past, and the one to the future, and be present, right at this very second. Feel the temperature in your mouth — is it cold and refreshing or warm and comforting? Is the food spicy or bland? Is it hot or bearable? Is it crispy, soft, chewy? Are there different textures? What are the flavours, the tastes, the aromas? Which flavour is subtle or strong? Is it balanced?

Have you ever thought that you are analysing and asking yourself unconsciously this multitude of questions within few seconds? And the ultimate one, the only one you answer spontaneously: is it good?

Define good! Is it pleasant? Exceptional? Rare? Out of the world? Decadent, delicious, scrumptious, divine, exquisite, sensual, nourishing, addictive? Do you want more or have you had enough? Is it too rich? Is it too complex? Are there too many flavours contradicting each other? Would you eat it often or just once in a while? That is a decision you make within seconds too.

How amazing! You live in an era when you have too many alternatives, too many dilemmas: it takes ages to determinate to go that way or the other way. But when it comes to food, you make a brutal judgement, an instinctive visceral choice, not a meditated one.

This book is about pleasure, sensuality, rediscovering the emotions food can bring you. It is a collection of short stories, memories, dreams, tales, myths and recipes that show ingredients under a kaleidoscopic light. After reading them, you will never think about vanilla, lemon or chocolate the same way: they will have a magical dimension, they will forever be alive in your mind.

Genesis

When did this all start? Women in my family are great cooks but not good bakers. I don't know if it's because they don't have a sweet tooth or if it's just not important to them. Nevertheless, I always dreamt about having a grandmother who would bake scrumptious fruit tarts and make jams in a copper pot. Instead of that both my grandmothers would eventually make an apple tart for family lunches, delicious I must say, but I was seeking something else, having a romantic image in my mind of a spacious stone kitchen, with a large chimney and an antique stove. I was imagining the aromas filling the room, watching them baking in a ballet that only home cooks can dance.

My mother doesn't bake either: the only dessert she ever made is a two-ingredients chocolate mousse, from a recipe she found on the wrapping of a supermarket chocolate bar. It is divine though, the best I ever tasted, and the angular stone of my pâtisserie education. I learnt to make it very early in life, and now my daughter is making it with pride and great success.

So feeling robbed of something I should have had during my childhood, I decided to start baking when my daughter was born: she would not have a Mamie Gâteaux but at least she would have the cakes, desserts, delicacies that I missed so much as a child.

I would bake with her, a toddler, sitting on the kitchen floor with the bowl between her legs, pouring the ingredients I had weighed, and stirring them clumsily with a wooden spoon, grabbing a mouthful of the mix from time to time, smiling at me, her cute face covered with chocolate.

Then we went from easy recipes to more elaborate ones, and I always let her help in the best way she could. There's a chocolate cake I bake often but most importantly every year for her birthday since she was born. It has been twenty-two years now, and she wouldn't have any other cake for the celebration of her life — it became a tradition, and I am pretty sure she will make it every year for her children's birthdays, when she has them.

I feel proud. I did achieve something: I may not have been able to give her roots, but at least she has something to relate to, a kind of family history, starting with me, like our surname. I created a gourmet ritual around every celebration — for example petits sablés and chocolate truffles for Christmas. We have to make them, otherwise it doesn't feel like Christmas.

It is even more important for us, as now we live in Australia and have for several years, to celebrate our French heritage through food, remembering the good old days when we were living in Paris.

We live in a society where enjoying the pleasure of epicurism is regarded as a privilege when it is really accessible to everyone. You only need to want it and not surrender to the cheap products that will not nourish nor fulfil you.

Harmony and contrast are the two essential elements of delectation in cuisine. You can be served an average dish, disgusting even, made with very expensive ingredients, as you can enjoy the bliss of a very simple meal made with fresh affordable local products. It is not a matter of money, nor education, it is just a question of taste and love you put in your cooking.

People are mostly divided in two groups, on one side the ones eating whatever they find, GMO's, over processed food, junk food, and on the other side you have the "health conscious", eating organic, drinking green juices. All of them are highly judgemental towards the other ones. But there is a category which is missing, or should I say dying: the "bons vivants", the epicureans, the ones who love good high quality food and know how to get pleasure out of it.

That is why I want to take you on a journey, discovering the pleasure of eating, everything, in moderation. Savour a glass of Champagne, a decadent chocolate dessert, the tang of citrus, the power of herbs and spices, let the flavours and aromas invade you and fill you with an extreme satisfaction.

There is no guilt, I am French, moderation is my philosophy... make the most of it, every bite is an infinite source of pleasure, envy, lust and love.

I am going to disseminate the seeds of delectation now, sharing my knowledge and my recipes with you, explaining, describing the taste of ingredients, picturing how it does feel to really experience pleasure, teaching an epicurism. I am going to drag you in my world of emotions, sensuality, dreams, travels, through stories, memories, myths, fables and tales.

Ritual

My ritual is in place, the blackcurrant-cinnamon-chocolate incense consuming itself in its Ganesh holder, a reddish wooden Buddha statue staring at me, or is it me looking at his peaceful appearance, praying for inspiration?

Few hours ago, I had an entire exciting book written in my mind, ideas dancing and jumping around, my thoughts wandering in the land of creativity while I was dozing in bed. As soon as I decided to get up and face reality, they abandoned me, leaving me in the cold placid world of practicality.

What did I want to put on paper? I can't even remember — a vicious amnesia is holding my brain hostage — and now, I am mourning this piece of myself forever lost in the abyss of my subconscious.

Alchemist of Flavours

I am impatient. I have been calling him many times, but he is not here yet. Is he avoiding me? Will he come? I know he's rude, late, unreliable, indifferent to my needs, letting me down so often, disillusioned and insecure. I admit it: I am under his influence. He put a powerful spell on me.

Without him I would be nothing, insignificant. Only *he* has the key to the secret energy Nature contains, the knowledge which can't be found in any books. He owns my heart. His murmur, exquisite poison, is running through my veins, taking possession of my thoughts insidiously. He is my addiction.

Where does this sweet melody come from? Blessed dream, I wake up finding him by my side, smiling at me.

"Stay with me my love! I would give up my soul to spend more time with you."

I beg him to hold me tight so I can finally let go and indulge in all the pleasures of the world. And we make a pact.

"Inspire me my beautiful angel!"

I don't feel him penetrating my soul as I am too busy in my quest for the essence of Truth, focusing on creating a singular moment of happiness, calling the Grace. I don't realise I am invoking him and inviting his erratic behaviour into my life. He asks me to serve him, to let his greatness infuse my mind, giving me glimpses of eternal Light.

All the wait, the despair, the sleepless nights, feeling the anxiety and the emptiness when he is not here, the emotional torture — all of these are worth it when he whispers to me: "See how everything is easy, my darling. The fulfilment you dreamt about so many times is just at your fingertips. You will complete your task and transform it to a Chef d'Oeuvre thanks to your dedication. It is for the greater good, to bring joy to Earth, that you will put your life into my hands." I work every night for him and for every wish granted he consumes a portion of my life span.

My muscles start relaxing, my breath slowing down, my heart beating in a voodoo mystical rhythm. It is so tempting, reaching all I ever wished for…I let him guide my actions, tearing away the secrecy, inventing a magical formula, sprinkling a little bit of this and a little bit of that into the scrumptious potion on the stove.

I don't see him disappearing. Once left alone in the dawn, I have accomplished my goal, acquired the perfect balance between the elements. Everything falls into place and culminates in a lustful sensation. Nothing to be altered, it is a piece of heaven sent to me, the nectar from the gods. Under his lead, I am an alchemist of flavours.

Now you know my secret. I have a demonic, cruel lover, torturing me and playing with me. He is an unfaithful enchanter, a dark magician ruling my hours. But I love him passionately and he brings the best out of me. It would be pretentious to think I owned him when I should only be devoted to him. He has many forms, is never expected, never to be conquered. He can abandon me at any moment and take himself off to a more exciting mistress. But I gave myself entirely to him and he left an indelible print in my existence. He is the one whistling me divine recipes. He has many names: Art, Talent, Muse, Inspiration…call him and one day he may appear by surprise.

Creation

Most pastry chefs do trials when they create a recipe, until they reach the combination they are after. For me it doesn't work like that. I think about some flavours, what I would like to do with them, which dessert I want to bring to life, and dream about the taste it must have, a perfect balance that brings certain emotions. So here I am, for weeks, sometimes for months, with an idea spinning in my head but reluctant to properly reveal itself to me. I am frustrated, impatient, trying to create new flavours, perfect ones, to play with the balance of spices, with the sweet and savoury. Where my imagination goes when I have to give a name for each fusion, drawing a fascination from faraway countries. Then one night, because it always happens when I don't expect it, a formula comes to me, and I know. I know this is the recipe I am looking for. I have no doubt about it. I get up in the morning, go into the kitchen and start measuring the ingredients the way it has been whistled to me. I am excited and scared. What if it doesn't work? Then comes the moment to taste my new creation, a bit apprehensive though confident in my gift, because this is a present from the gods. And it is beautiful, exactly what I wanted, what I fantasised about for so long, it gives me an ecstatic pleasure.

I go exactly through the same process with my writing. I think I want to talk about a certain ingredient, about how I could incorporate it in a story, a myth or as a character. I try to break down the flavours, the aromas, which one is strong, which one is subtle, and what I experience when I eat this food. And I will be stuck for days, not finding the right words, description, fable. But what is the story, the tale, the legend existing within me? I can't put my finger on it. It is still somewhere in my gut, maturing slowly, and it will come to me only when it will be ripe as a fruit under the sun. I must not chase it or it will hide even deeper and deeper, scared to be caught, too shy to be brought to light so soon. Therefore I will wait, with faith and conviction that sooner or later I will have its beauty, its uniqueness, and, at the very moment I am about to give up, everything comes to order. Sometimes it's close to what I expected, other times it's totally different — I even ended up starting writing about one subject and the finished allegory was about an unforeseen ingredient. I guess now that trying to force this won't get me anywhere: that a text, like a recipe, will just appear to me at an unpredictable time, already completed in the depths of my mind — as long as I am in a state of absolute awareness. And then it will start all over again with another component, the chasing, the wait, the illumination. That is the beautifully painful process called Creation.

Reminiscence

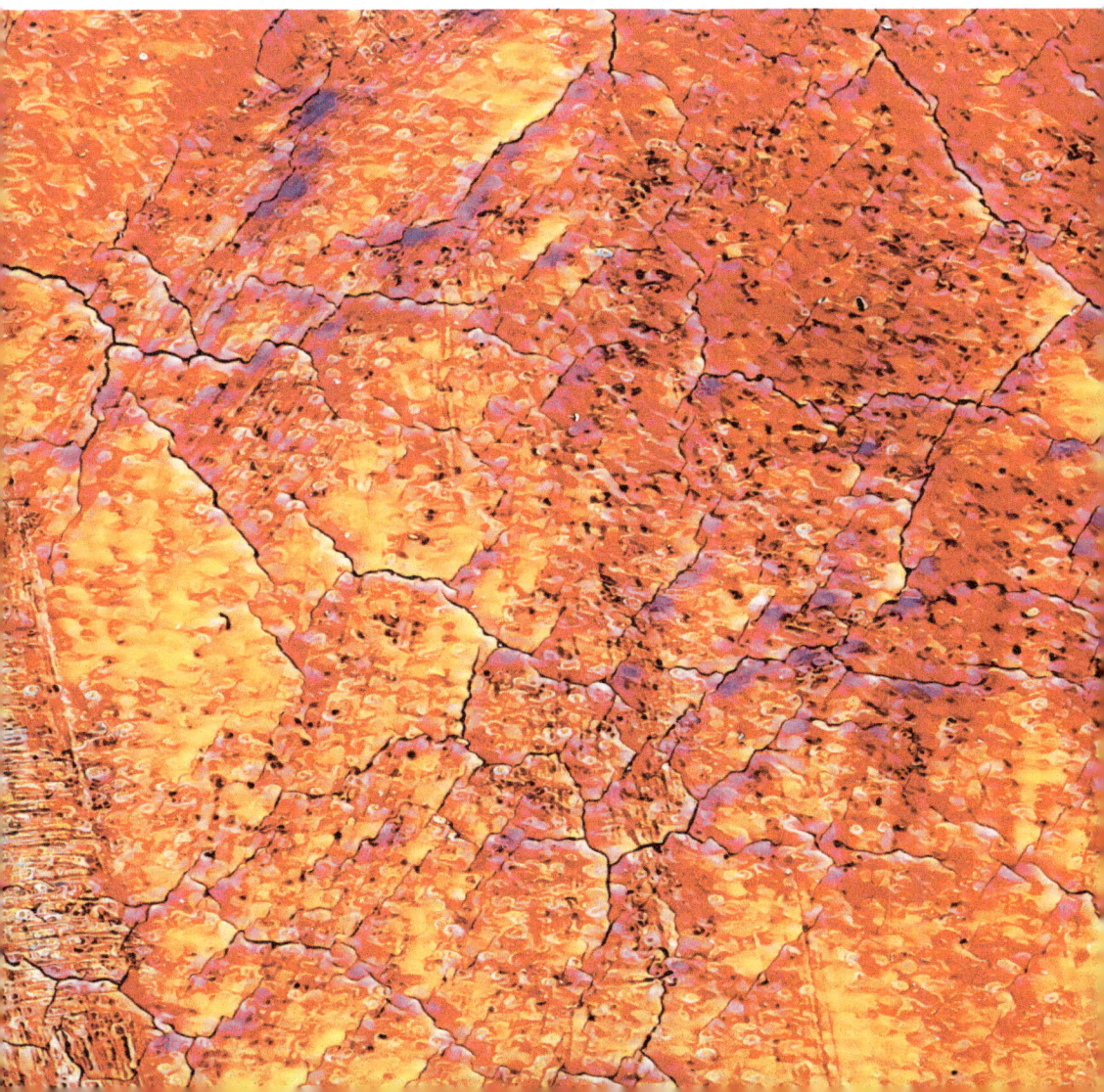

Pain Perdu (Stale Bread)

That year's Christmas celebrations were full of joy. All the family was reunited, counting their blessings despite the terrible famine they had suffered in the months before. The priest joined them for Twelfth Night, bringing them some delicacies to share. There were enough victuals to call it a banquet: a thick vegetable soup with morsels of lard, several loaves of bread, some cheese, wine, apples and even a roast, which was a real luxury.

In this glacial winter morning, life was back to normal. The men were away at the fair trying to sell the calf and they wouldn't be back before late at night. She had already collected the nourishing milk warm from the cow and gathered the perfect just-laid eggs from the coop. She was about to start preparing a stew for dinner with the feast's leftovers when her gaze stopped at the stale loaf sitting on the buffet.

– What a pity! Me alive, God forbid there will be any waste in this house!

But she had to eat something during the day anyway. The crumb was too hard and really dry, so she decided to do a little experiment. She grabbed a bowl, poured the creamy white milk in it, cracked an egg over it, the vibrant orangeish shade of the yolk mixing beautifully with the pure snow of the milk. She then cut two slices of the stale bread, not without struggling, and soaked them in the liquid. She put the cast iron pan on the wood burning stove, which was lit night and day to keep the small place heated; added a dash of butter and threw in the simmering chestnut fat the now soft pieces. She let them gently fry until they got golden on both sides. She picked them up delicately, disposed them on a plate, sat at the rustic table, and, uncertain of the success of the recipe, but happy that at least she'd have a full stomach, she took a bite.

– Not so bad! But it's lacking something…

She then remembered the little jar of honey Father Mathieu gave her to relieve her sore throat, that precious elixir…and decided to drizzle some on her new culinary creation. When she tasted it, she reached the idea of perfection. It was warm, comforting, decadent even. The little bit of added sweetness brought her so much contentment that she forgot she was in her small country farm, where kitchen, living and bed spaces were one and the same room. She closed her eyes and started dreaming of damasks, velvets and silks, in a bourgeois townhouse, enjoying a life of leisure. Instead of working with bare hands in her icy land of desolation, she could see herself seated on a cosy armchair, she could feel the flames of the fireplace invading her veins, she could taste the wine she would drink while conversing with acquaintances, holding a "salon" renowned for her art of causerie. At the last bite, she wasn't hungry any more — she had eaten all of it, she wanted more of the soaked pain perdu! She was experiencing for the first time in her life how it felt to eat for pleasure and not for necessity. She had discovered the exquisite sin called Gourmandise.

Pain Perdu

4 slices of stale bread
300 millilitres milk (or almond milk)
1 egg
Vanilla sugar
Honey
Berries

Le pain perdu and clafoutis were originally dishes made by the poor to avoid wasting food at a time when sustenance was very rare. Those dishes are fundamentals of my French roots and culture. At home, we don't decide to make pain perdu unless there is actually some stale bread about to go to the bin. Same for clafoutis: it is baked only to use overripe fruit. It is totally inconceivable for me and my family and friends in France too, to order French toast in a café or a restaurant, to pay for what should be a leftover dish and which is actually not made with stale bread, but with fresh, or a buttery brioche. Leave the brioche alone! Don't spoil it in this recipe! Le Pain Perdu should be a homemade recipe, enjoyed at home only: it can be for breakfast, afternoon tea or dessert. It is amazing how a dish for the poor became a fancy dessert.

Clafoutis

To prepare luscious clafoutis, you need to gather 500 grams of ripe juicy Burgundy-wine coloured cherries. Gently wash them under cool water, pat them delicately with a soft cloth, remove their little cheeky tails but keep the pits in the fruits as they infuse more flavour into the dessert. Place the flamboyant cherries in an old-fashioned porcelain or clay dish that you will have previously brushed with unsalted, creamy butter.

Sprinkle the cherries with two tablespoons of sugar, caressing them amorously so they are evenly sweetened.

Turn on the oven at 180 degrees Celsius.

In a bowl, whisk together two tablespoons of voluptuous double cream, two tablespoons of devilish sugar, three tablespoons of unflavoured oil and three tablespoons of vaporous cornflour.

Add to the concoction three rich-coloured egg yolks and mix until beautifully combined.

Then beat the whites until they reach delicate snow peaks.

Incorporate with love the aerial whites, slowly, from the bottom of the bowl to the top, in a smooth circular motion.

Pour cautiously the lavish foamy batter over the cherries, and let the magic happen in the oven for 30 minutes, until the clafoutis shows an appealing dark golden tan.

Let it cool down, allowing the aromas and flavours to be sublimed, and the texture to set and embrace the cherries.

Savour this delectable dessert still warm to enjoy its distinctive comforting deliciousness.

Clafoutis aux Cerises

500 grams cherries
2 tablespoons double cream
2 tablespoons vanilla sugar
3 tablespoons oil
3 tablespoons cornflour
3 eggs

FOR THE CLAY DISH
2 tablespoons sugar
Unsalted butter

Tarte aux Pommes

There is something incredibly warm and comforting in Grandma's kitchen. It is not only a room where we cook and bake and eat. There is this special atmosphere as if time had stopped, and as soon as I step in, I feel surrounded by love and memories. It has a soul: her soul.

The soft golden light piercing from outside through the windows, dressed with crochet curtains. The imposing, immaculate porcelain sink, with underneath this red and white Vichy fabric hiding the soaps, sponges, bucket and other cleaning products. The wooden bench on which is sitting a large dark green pot containing spoons, ladles and whisks. The rustic table with always, at the centre, a bowl full of seasonal fruits in case someone needs a collation. The not-that-straight shelves with a few clay baking dishes of different shapes and sizes. The reddish shiny copper pots and pans hanging from the ceiling. The heavy cast iron stove taking most of the space, proud of its importance.

There are no or almost no modern tools. No dishwasher, no mixer, no coffee machine, no fancy fridge with the family's to-do lists and timetables, just the robust one she bought in the 1950's… It is timeless, beautiful with simplicity and savoir-faire.

It is travelling in time by taking the time, remembering every single one of her movements. I take her apron, which is folded on a chair, wrap it around my waist. The flour jar is still where it used to be; I grab it and gather the other ingredients.

I put the flour on the bench, make a well in the middle, add a bit of salt. Slowly I pour the water while mixing with one hand, not too much, until there are no dry bits any more. And I knead, constantly, putting all my strength in my arms, the dough becomes elastic and has this soft skin like a baby's bum. I roll it into a ball, mark a cross with a knife; it's opening like a flower. "Don't forget the cross, she used to say, or the magic won't operate." I cover it with a tea towel and set it aside to rest.

Now to the butter. I lay it on the table and start beating it with the rolling pin until it's flat, then put it back in the fridge.

As the dough has relaxed, I can roll it down in a rectangle as Grandma taught me. I put the sheet of butter on two thirds of it and fold everything together, one third on the top of the middle part, then the last third. I turn it of one quarter on the right then I roll carefully — "Make sure not to break the dough, sweetheart; you build layers, do not let them mix" — fold it again and put the pastry in the fridge.

I place some glass jars in a large pot filled with water and bring it to the boil. They sit there for quite a while until I remove them carefully and dispose them upside down on a clean tea towel.

I grab a saucepan from the ceiling, pour in some sugar and head straight to the stove, medium heat — "let it melt, do not stir, it will caramelise by itself". I take a second saucepan, pour in the cream and put it on the heat while I am cutting the butter. Now the cream is warm enough, I drizzle it on the golden caramel little by little, stirring with a wooden spoon, with extreme caution, as it's bubbling like a volcano in eruption. I remove the pot from the heat, add the cubes of butter, whisk until it's combined and here comes the most important part of the task. I take off the lid of the beautiful bucolic sea salt container she bought on the

French West Coast, and count the pinches of fleur de sel I put in the caramel…one, two, three, four, five…"don't forget to taste"… one more, six! It's perfect, just like hers.

I fill the jars with the precious liquid, close them, and let them cool down.

It's time to make some turns to the pastry: I roll it, fold it, turn it one quarter on the right, roll it again, fold it again and back to the fridge.

How long have I been in the kitchen? Two hours only! It feels like an eternity without Grandma telling me all the stories of her childhood.

I'd better start peeling the fruits. I choose the apples like a connoisseur, not too sweet, not too acid, remove their skin, cut them in quarters, slice them.

"Haven't you forgotten something, darling?"

Right! Where is the lemon? I cut it in half and drizzle some of its juice on the apples so they don't turn brown.

I turn the oven on — "Very hot, otherwise the pastry will not rise." I fetch the pastry, give it one more turn and roll it thin. The cutters are on the shelves near the baking dishes; I choose a large one and a small one — "One for everybody and an extra little one for my commis, love." I always felt so privileged and important to have one just for me. I cut a sheet of baking paper, lay it on the tray, dispose the circles of pastry on it and then arrange my apple slices in a beautiful rosace. Straight in the oven. And now the wait starts. How did she know without a window when it was ready? "Don't open the door, it will let the heat escape." Fifteen minutes, she said, the time to make a cup of tea and drink it slowly. I will do that then. As soon as I finish I reach the oven door, open it, and I feel this warm feeling invading me — she is here with me, without her the tarts wouldn't look so perfect. I start doubting, maybe she is still alive, maybe she is in the other room and will come in a few seconds…

I place the burning tray carefully on the wooden bench, and reality hits me — she is not coming back. I go to the buffet, choose her favourite plate and dispose my little pâtisserie on it, sprinkle some icing sugar, open a jar of salted butter caramel just warm, drizzle it all over my Tarte aux Pommes, and look at it. It is astonishing, delicate, an image out of a book. With the silver cutlery I cut a piece and bring it to my mouth, and I am eight years old again: it is warm, delicious, sweet with this little salty note.

"Mmmm, Grandma you're the best! Will you always bake these for me?"

"Yes, sweetie. But someday I will have to go to heaven, so you will have to make it yourself. Don't worry, I will stay by your side and whisper you the recipe."

Full Butter Puff Pastry

400 grams strong flour
2 grams salt
Around 200 millilitres cold water
300 grams unsalted butter
100 grams slightly salted butter

The dough should match the butter consistency, and must be kept covered.

Cold water is essential: use ice cubes if necessary to bring it under 10 degrees Celsius.

Take your time: puff pastry requires lots of patience and shouldn't be rushed.

Do not roll more than twice, and put the pastry back in the fridge between turns. A full butter puff pastry requires six turns (and not more than two at a time).

The slightly salted butter is good for this recipe; if you want to use puff pastry for another recipe, switch to a full amount of unsalted butter.

A cold environment is better for the success of this recipe, otherwise the butter will soften too quickly.

Bake in a very hot oven (220 degrees Celsius), otherwise the butter will melt before the pastry rises.

Salted Butter Caramel

300 grams white sugar
300 millilitres whipping cream
225 grams unsalted butter
5 or 6 pinches fleur de sel

Caramelise the sugar in a large saucepan.

Heat the cream then pour it little by little into the caramel on low heat.

Take off the heat and add the butter sliced in cubes while continuously mixing with a wooden spoon. Add the salt according to your taste.

Another delicious version of Tarte aux Pommes can be made using the almond short pastry recipe (page 147). Layer it with apple-pear puree (page 134), then cover the puree with apple slices and sprinkle them with vanilla sugar before baking.

Grandma's Remedy

There is something magical about grandmothers' remedies; sipping the warm delicious liquid cure, I am remembering the time when instead of popping a pill, a loving old lady used all her ancestral knowledge to help me get over a cold, a flu or a bronchitis. Sometimes it was enjoyable such as drinking this beautiful mixture of lemon, honey and rum in hot water. Other times it was painful, like the mustard cataplasm applied on my chest for hours, burning memories of a tough night, but I would wake up feeling much better, and it was way more efficient than the Vicks my mum would use.

How strange it is to realise that it is not the years which mean I'm ageing, but knowing that my childhood is a long-lost epoch and that those simple but extraordinary human beings will never be part of my life again. All I have from them now is a little reminder that I will not allow to die — I transmit it to my daughter, as it has been transmitted for generations.

I have heard stories too of incredible women in my family long gone before I was born. My great-grandmother Marie-Antoinette saved my grandmother Marcelle, two years old, from the typhus during World War I, putting her back on her breast as she was feeding her second child, and on top of the mother's milk she would give her some kind of spirit; I think it was rum.

My grandmother put her premature son in a shoebox filled with cotton to keep him warm and fed him with bananas. He became a tall strong man.

I feel nostalgic and sad that their lives will be forgotten, that we will remember some anecdotes for few generations and then they too will disappear as if they had never existed.

It is the same concerning traditional cuisine: we are loosing our roots, our culture, in an era when everything must go fast, including cooking, and must be appealing to the eye instead of being of the highest quality, nourishing and tasting good. We don't take the time to eat any more. Where are those interminable Sunday family lunches, when I played with my cousins while the adults were staying at the table for five or six hours, drinking a bit too much and debating politics? When my grandmother would put me on her knees and sing me a song from the Northern French folklore about little Jesus going to school, carrying his cross on his shoulders? Can I remember all the lyrics? Almost. Although I sang it to my daughter when she was a child, I have to do it for my grandchildren for them to know where they are coming from. Especially when living in another country, it is crucial to pass on those little things to recall who we are in a time of global existential crisis.

And it is the same with my Italian heritage — although I can still understand the language, I am too shy to speak it now, which is funny knowing I could speak Italian before French. Clémence, my daughter never wanted to learn it, but she has the temper and the love of food. That she is proud of.

So here I am, in bed, with the presages of a cold, drinking my Grog, knowing I don't need anything else, that I will sweat during the night, and wake up much better in the morning. And I will keep on drinking it twice a day for one or two days, until I completely recover.

Grog

Now to make a beautiful Grog: put the kettle on. Squeeze a large lemon in a mug, add one or two teaspoons of honey according to your taste, pour the hot water and add a good lid of rum. I use dark rum in which I put a vanilla pod to infuse for several months — it gives to it an incomparable flavour. Stir, drink while it's still very hot, and don't forget to enjoy, and go to bed for a well-deserved sleep.

The Maid

Madeleine is terrified. She is just a maid — how could she live up to the Polish king's expectations? She is not a pastry chef — the bad tempered cook fought with the steward and left with all the desserts — so how could she replace him and satisfy the court with her humble cakes? But here she is, in charge of the collation, and she's lost in the marquise's kitchen, scratching her head, desperately looking for a miracle. All she can bake is peasant recipes, ingredients put together in two minutes, nothing glorious, although deliciously fulfilling.

She doesn't have a choice; she has to serve something. There is no point in trying to replicate desserts she hasn't even tasted — that would be a complete disaster. She'd better stick to the only recipe she knows.

She gathers the ingredients and looks for little tins, but she can't find any. It has to be elegant, not a family cake cut in pieces. Her gaze stops at the empty scallop shells. That could do it. She cautiously cleans them with soap and rinses them thoroughly, dries them and coats them with soft butter.

She puts some butter to melt in a saucepan on the immense stove, sieves the flour with a little bit of baking powder, leaves it aside. She chooses two big beautiful eggs that she cracks in a bowl, then adds some sugar and whisks energetically until the mix becomes whitish and foamy. She then adds the flour and baking powder while constantly stirring. She pours the lukewarm melted butter and keeps on folding the batter. It is too simple, not flavoursome enough. She grabs a lemon and decides to perfume the mixture with its zest.

She then fills the scallop shells, not too much, so the cakes will nicely rise without overflowing.

She has some time: the guests are not ready yet, and those cakes are way better warm just out of the oven. She puts the improbable moulds on the side, on a bed of ice, in order to clean the kitchen. She will just have to bake them for a few minutes and then go back to her daily chores.

After some time, she puts them in the very hot oven. Surprisingly, after few minutes a big bump appears on the top of them. A little bit disappointed she places the little teacakes on a silver platter, and makes her way to the garden.

As she is serving them, she is called out by a mature man, very important, given the way the other people address him. Her heart stops; she's shaking, certain of his disappointment and that she will be fired straight away. She is shyly approaching.

"Yes, My Lord...?"

"I just wanted to compliment the chef. Those cakes are delicious, light, buttery and this subtle fragrance of citrus is paradisiac. How do you call those scrumptious nibbles?"

"They don't have a name, My Lord, we just bake them in my family."

"We must find them an appellation — what is your name, child?"

"Madeleine, My Lord."

"That's settled, from now on they will be referred as madeleines, a souvenir of an ingenious little maid."

Madeleine timidly bows out and runs back to the kitchen, still in shock, stupefied by what she just heard. She, an insignificant Lorraine maid, has been praised for her cooking. What she doesn't know yet is that she, her recipe and her little town Commercy will be famous worldwide for the centuries to come.

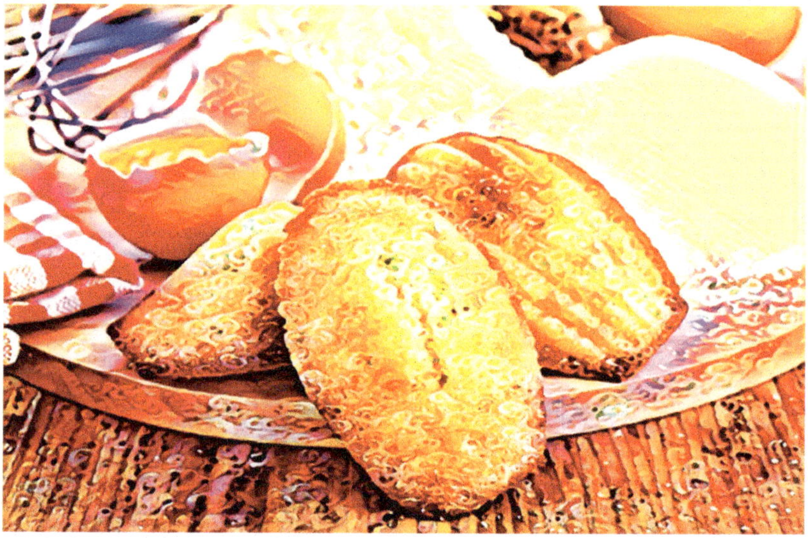

Madeleines

100 grams flour
3 grams baking powder (small teaspoon)
100 grams unsalted butter
2 large eggs (70 grams each)
110 grams sugar
1 large lemon

Sift the flour and the baking powder. Melt the butter in a saucepan on low heat. Zest the lemon. Whip the eggs and the sugar for around five minutes so it's well aerated and whitish. Sprinkle the flour/baking soda on top of it; while mixing, add the melted butter and the lemon zest. Pour into greased madeleines moulds to two-thirds full. Put the madeleines tins in the fridge for half an hour to two hours. Preheat the oven at 220 degrees Celsius. Bake it for four minutes, then reduce the temperature to 200 degrees for four more minutes.

Of course in the eighteenth century baking powder didn't exist, but as I don't know what amount of yeast was used nor when it was incorporated into the batter, I deliberately made the choice to leave this historic incoherence in the story, for the sake of the recipe.

Time Machine

I am mourning my childhood, my innocence, my dreams, illusions and hopes.

I am mourning the time gone, lost, wasted.

I am mourning the happy moments, the ones when I wanted to stop time so they would last forever.

Nostalgia squeezes me as I look at old photos, remembering what has been and is no more.

Loss and emptiness fill my heart. I am drowning in the void of unreachable desires.

Only my senses can awaken me to the joy of souvenirs, triggering sensations that I thought were forever gone, the same way that the fragrance of a stranger in the street captures my imagination and reminds me so vividly of the delightful bliss of nesting my nose in my lover's neck.

Food is a wonderful time machine, bringing me back to an exquisite dimension, where my senses are stimulated by the colours, shapes, aromas, scents, flavours, and textures, so that I am physically and emotionally transported.

I get to relive the reassuring comfort of Grandma's kitchen, watching her making gnocchi and apple tart with so much confidence in each of her movements that I already knew the meal will be delicious as usual. Recalling with emotion the first time I ate a fresh-milky fig my man lovingly harvested for me from his garden after a passionate night. It wasn't just about the fig; it was about this beautiful weekend spent in his retreat, being happy with each other's company, when our love was still new and exciting, when he still thought I was the most wonderful woman on earth, the best thing that ever happened to him.

The first sweet juicy cherry of the year is the promise of a beautiful summer, filled with clafoutis, sunshine and quality time with my daughter being cheeky.

My heart then fills itself with reverie, fragile hopefulness that nothing is ever lost, that those happy moments will always be alive in the infinite essence of me.

He Was Like Chocolate

He was like chocolate,
All sweet at the beginning,
Then bittersweet.
Finally he turned dark bitter.
Like chocolate,
She couldn't stop craving him,
Going back to him with the hope
That he would be sweet again.

He was like chocolate, all sweet at the beginning, worshipping her, showering her with loving words and gestures. Then he became bittersweet — he would from time to time give her all of him, and from time to time hurt her, pushing her away. Her heart broke, but her love for him never failed, as long as he was loving, even sporadically. Finally he turned to dark bitter, acting cold all the time. He lied, cheated and disrespected her.

Like chocolate, she couldn't stop craving him. She still loved him with passion, she still had hope. Weeks and months passed, she had her good and terrible moments, but tears ran down her cheeks almost every night. Life was getting gloomy and dull. Only his love could bring a smile back to her beautiful face; only he, could illuminate her eyes. Nothing could make her feel better than the embrace of his arms, the warmth of his touch and the sound of his voice. She was missing his love, which used to feel like a chocolate mousse caress, deliciously sweet, aerated and smooth.

As she had never been able to give up on chocolate, she wasn't able to give up on him. He was her addiction, even stronger than chocolate.

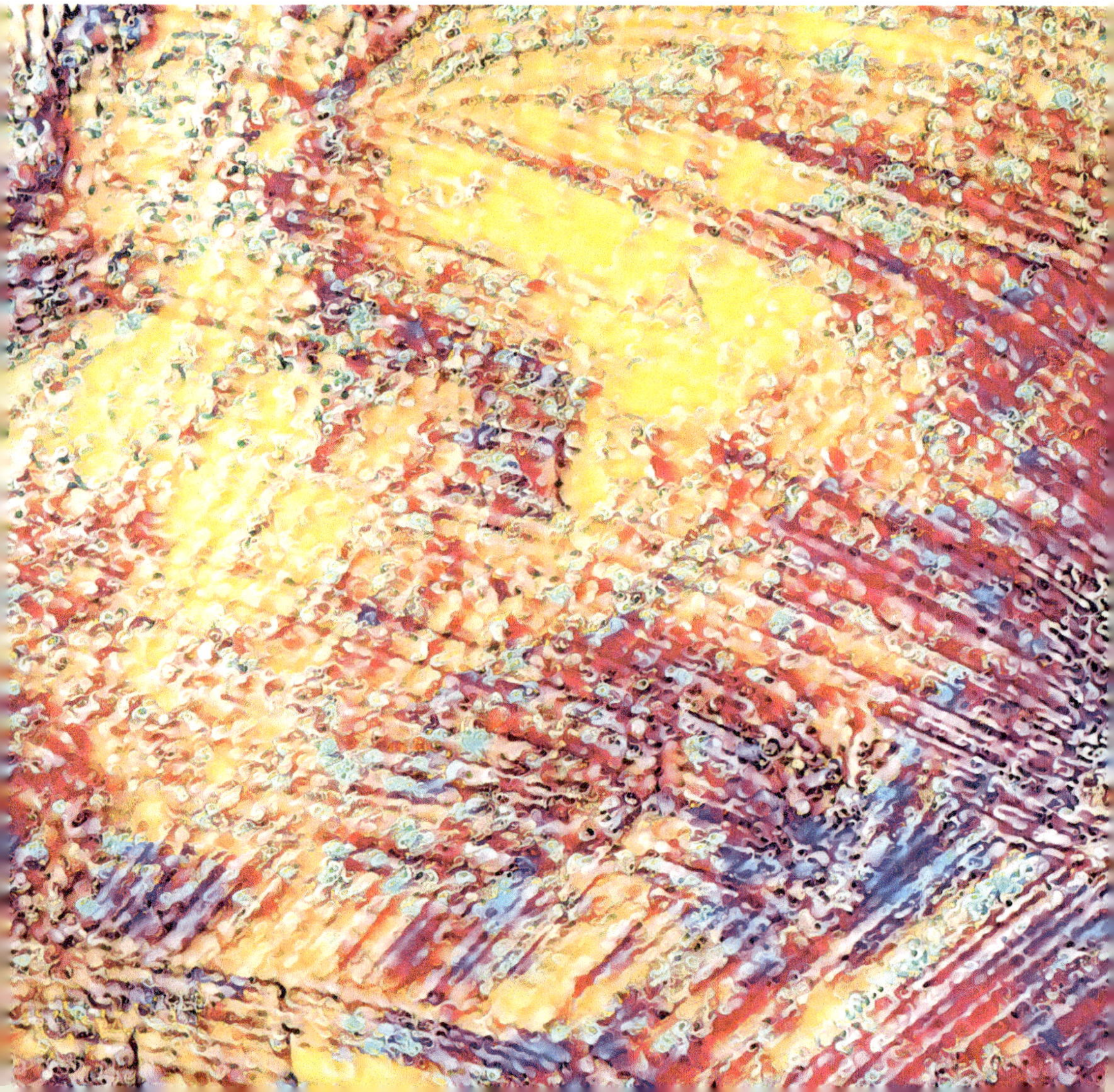

Whimsical

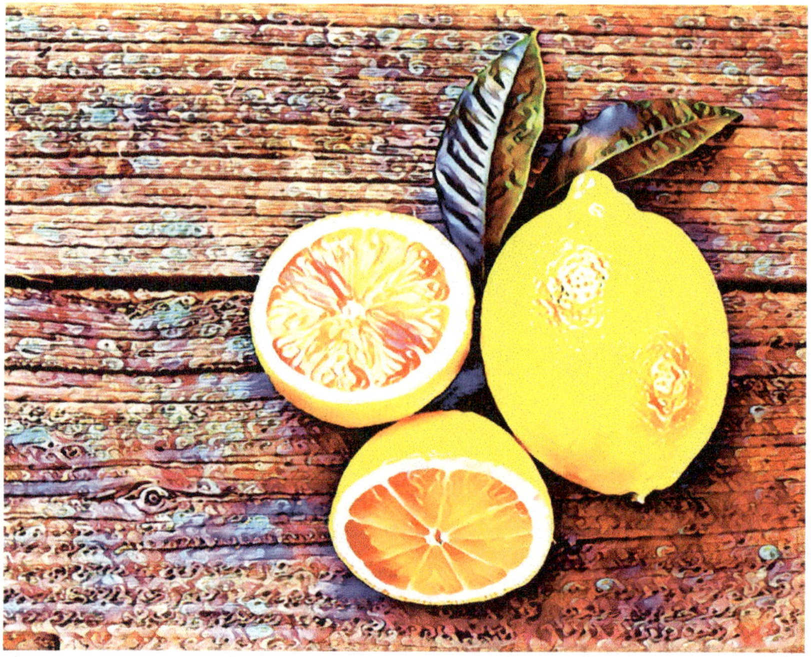

The Kitchen Goddess

When you see her, the first thing you notice is how vibrant she is. Her skin is glowing like sunshine, exhaling a subtle perfume like meadows. She is bubbly, fresh and full of life. But when you get to know her, you discover her ambivalence, the complex paradox in her, acting as a seductive woman teasing you then pushing you away with her tartness like a shy girl. This versatile enchantress loves games, playing with your senses, your feelings, your mind, inviting you to a dominant–submissive relationship where her sharp, tangy, acidic personality becomes almost unbearable… until she surrenders, finally giving you a glimpse of her soft side, dragging you to the land of juicy sweetness and delicate captivating scent.

Here stands the profound range of all her abilities to change under your touch, adapting herself to your deepest desires, bringing you infinite variations of emotions from the most decadent to the slightest. She makes you travel from a hot summer in Italy to a spring day galloping in an orange-blossom field, hair in the wind, a cool breeze caressing your face. Purely blissful, she gives you the chill, the adrenaline but also the comfort and relief. She is always exciting, never dull, a mistress owning your thoughts and leaving an unforgettable taste on your lips, an obsessive combination of sweet and sour. She is like a rose and its thorns.

She is not to be controlled, tamed only, with tact and savoir-faire. She erases boredom from your existence, relieves your thirst and enhances whatever she touches to the divine if handled wisely and with loving consciousness. Only then, she capitulates and leaves you in an ecstatic state. She is the goddess of your kitchen: she is the one you call Lemon.

We are all addicted to something. I don't know what it is for you, but that one thing I couldn't live without is lemon. The delicious citrusy smell, zest, lift, pep is so refreshing it gets my mind and body happy. I am really feeling down if I don't have my daily lemon fix. I love it so much that I use it everywhere and as much as I can. In many desserts, of course, and believe me I keep the tang and don't sweeten them much — what would be the point otherwise? If I don't bake, I squeeze lemon into cold water with ice cubes: this is the perfect drink, highly enjoyable and healthy. I also use lemon in my savoury dishes but mostly with poultry, although sautéed champignons and bacon enhanced with a bit of lemon juice to serve on top of a Gorgonzola and Riesling risotto is to die for.

Even the tea I drink is citrus based, the bergamot in Earl Grey makes me feel on holidays, the scent is delightful and always triggers sunny memories. It was hard for me to source a bergamot tree in Australia, but I finally found one. It is slowly growing in my tiny backyard, not giving that much fruit. I spend months looking at the little fruits with loving eyes, promise of pleasure growing slowly; but to my despair, the possums steal them as soon as they're about to be ripe. I could save only two of them last year. Sometimes I feel that I am at war with Nature. Slugs gorge on my lemons and Buddha's hand fruits as soon as they point out of the flower: it is extremely frustrating. Although I don't appreciate that much the flavour of the fruit itself, the peel is enchanting. I took the rind off, dried it and kept it aside so I could add it to some non-citrus tea I have.

Lemon has always been around me. My perfumes always have a citrus base, not only because they smell better to me, like being in a field, but also because other scents turn really bad on my skin, it's written in the stars, some kind of fate. And the combination of citrus and vanilla in a fragrance is exquisite. I thrive on lemon sorbet in summer or just suck lemon flesh itself.

Is it because of my Italian background that I need this gorgeous Mediterranean fruit to run deep in my veins, even if I was born and bred in Paris? What is it that makes it so addictive?

The Maya Vestal

Have you heard about this Maya vestal, virgin beauty wearing a delicate dress, vessel of the divinity of fertility? She was peacefully living in a secret forest for centuries, thriving, dedicating her life to the idol, magic fertilised to bring back the Mistress of Spices to earth; long time left alone, unbothered, hidden from the greed of humankind, until a man found her, despoiled her sanctuary, abducted her and took her far away.

Abandoned far from her mythical land she let herself waste, her loins stayed empty, she became fruitless, because she wasn't to be spoilt by the profane: forbidden to be touched, she had to stay pure, keeping herself for the sacred. She was missing her enchanted clearing, its soft light, the crystalline water, and was weakened by her inability to serve her goddess.

One day, a knight saw her, fell in love with her, and cared for her, watched over her, making sure she had all she needed, getting enough sun and shade, pure water and delicate food. He adored her. Slowly she softened, let him get closer; her figure was changing, she was coming back to life, and she allowed him to love her. Their bodies danced from dawn to dusk, her skin exhaling a mesmerising tropical scent.

Her mortal chevalier has joined the stars since a long time now. Torn between her promise to be faithful to him and her duty towards her godliness she has to stay intact, except in a yearly celebration when a beau with the purest soul will incarnate her lost lover, praying for the divine to happen.

If you are lucky, you can see the goddess walking through her Eden, her long bronze legs caressed by the sun, the warm breeze diffusing her bewitching fragrance, an aura of spicy aromas, subtle exotic reminders of her original home. If you talk to her with respect and devotion she may allow you to taste her lips, exhaling paradisiac flavours, promises of exquisite felicity. Her name is a metaphoric origin of the world: you call her Vanilla.

You can add a little bit of magic in your daily life. Every time you use a vanilla bean, instead of chucking it in the bin, just dry it with a tea towel and put it in a jug of sugar. Over time, all the flavours will infuse, and you'll have a delicious vanilla sugar that you can add to your coffee or tea, or use in your baking. Then you'll be transported to a faraway country, where the Maya vestal is longing for her lover's return.

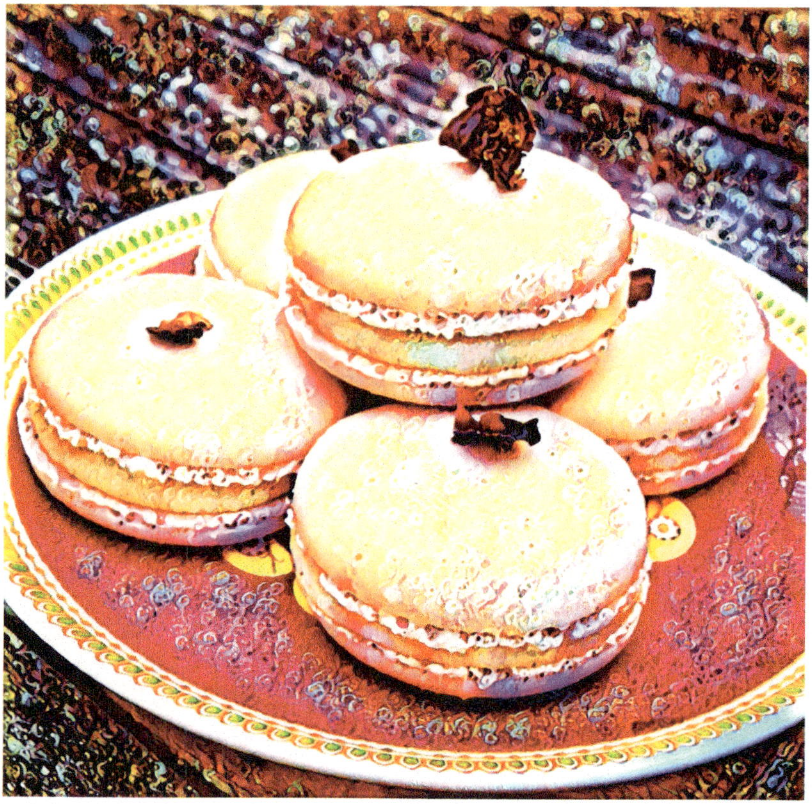

Origination by the Moon

The mineral ocean is calm; just a little curl is dancing on the pearly sand. As she is emerging out of the water, the iridescent blue moon illuminates her voluptuous hips. Glowing like an Aphrodite, standing nude, vulnerable in the immensity and the silence of this magnificent night, she wants to invoke her mother: the goddess of abundance.

"Ô Mother, opalescent enchantress, dressed in dazzling muslin, ripping through the sky, riding your silver chariot from one constellation to another, escaping the Sun, her husband, in an eternal race, stopping to silently caress with a loving gaze your lover, lost in an eternal sleep.

"Ô Mother, receptacle of life and universal fertility, you represent and glorify the fair sex in its beauty, complexity, sensibility and courage. The intensity of your glow inspired many legends. You are the creator of us all women, commanding the circle of life, every motion of the abysses including within female loins.

"Ô Mother, I am desperate, in the loneliness of my condition, searching for pure love since centuries, denied carnal pleasure and maternity by the gods themselves. My heart is cold and empty: even the freedom of crossing the seven seas is no longer enjoyable.

"Ô Mother, help me! Soothe my pain! Liberate me!"

Staring at her daughter with a tender eye, feeling the profound depth of her sorrow and moved in her maternal instinct, the lustrous satellite drops a tear, which falls into the hands of the mythical creature, perfectly rounded, glossy, the size of a gold coin. The maid takes a bite, exhaling a whisper of satisfaction. It is lightly crispy outside and chewy and deliciously moist inside.

This is how the moon created macarons.

Mistress of Spices Macarons

MACARONS SHELLS
300 grams almond meal
300 grams pure icing sugar
110 grams egg whites, preferably few days old
3 vanilla pods

FOR THE ITALIAN MERINGUE
300 grams caster sugar
80 millilitres water
110 grams egg whites, preferably few days old
Few drops of lemon juice

GANACHE
400 millilitres whipping cream
3 vanilla pods
1 Tonka bean
450 grams white couverture chocolate

MACARONS SHELLS
Combine almond meal and pure icing sugar together in a very large bowl. Split 3 vanilla pods in half lengthwise and scrape the grains to incorporate them into the mix. Add 110 grams egg whites and mix well until it becomes a sticky paste.

Pour the water and caster sugar into a saucepan and put it on medium heat. When it comes to a boil, put a sugar thermometer in it to monitor the temperature. Brush the sides of the pan with a wet brush to avoid crystallisation.

Meanwhile, put the 110 grams egg whites remaining in a mixer bowl, add few drops of lemon juice, and start mixing slowly.

When the syrup's temperature reaches 115 degrees Celsius, put the mixer bowl on high speed.

Once the syrup is at 118 degrees Celsius, take the pan off the heat, slow the mixer speed and slowly pour the syrup into the egg whites. Pour it down the sides of the bowl to avoid the whisk splashing sugar syrup and seriously burns you. This step done, put the mixer back on high speed for at least 2 minutes, to allow the meringue to cool down to 50 degrees Celsius.

Then mix the Italian meringue with the almond-sugar-vanilla paste with a spatula, in circle motions from bottom to top of the bowl. When ready, the mix should be glossy and form ribbons when lifted (not too thick, not too runny).

Prepare a baking tray with baking paper on it.

Prepare a large pastry bag with an 11 tip. Fill it with the mix and start pipping, allowing enough space as it will spread.

Gently tap the baking tray against the bench to eliminate air bubbles.

You can sprinkle one side with Dutch cacao for decorating.

Let it sit until a shell doesn't stick to your finger when touched. I would recommend to do this process with the air conditioning on, especially here in Australia where humidity is macarons' worst nightmare.

Preheat your oven between 130 and 160 degrees Celsius. All ovens are different and only after few trials will you know which temperature works best.

Bake the shells for 10 to 12 minutes. From experience, if they don't crack by minute 7, they won't crack.

Allow the shells to cool down before removing them from the baking paper.

GANACHE

Pour the whipping cream into a saucepan. Split 3 vanilla beans lengthwise with a paring knife, add the grains to the cream. Grate a Tonka bean over the cream. Bring the cream to a boil, turn off the heat, cover the saucepan and let the flavours infuse for half an hour to an hour.

Melt the white couverture chocolate over a bain marie.

Strain the cream through a sieve to remove the vanilla beans.

Make sure the cream is still hot before pouring it slowly over the melted chocolate.

Mix until perfectly combined.

Pour the ganache into a shallow dish so it will set faster. Air conditioning will help too. I found that it would take ages to set in the fridge and then suddenly harden too much.

Try to match your macaron shells by pair. Prepare a piping bag with a 9 tip, fill it with ganache, and pipe. Leave room on the side of the shell as it will spread when covered with the second shell.

Put the macarons in the fridge for at least 24 hours. It's when the aromas will beautifully combine.

Enjoy those morsels of happiness at room temperature.

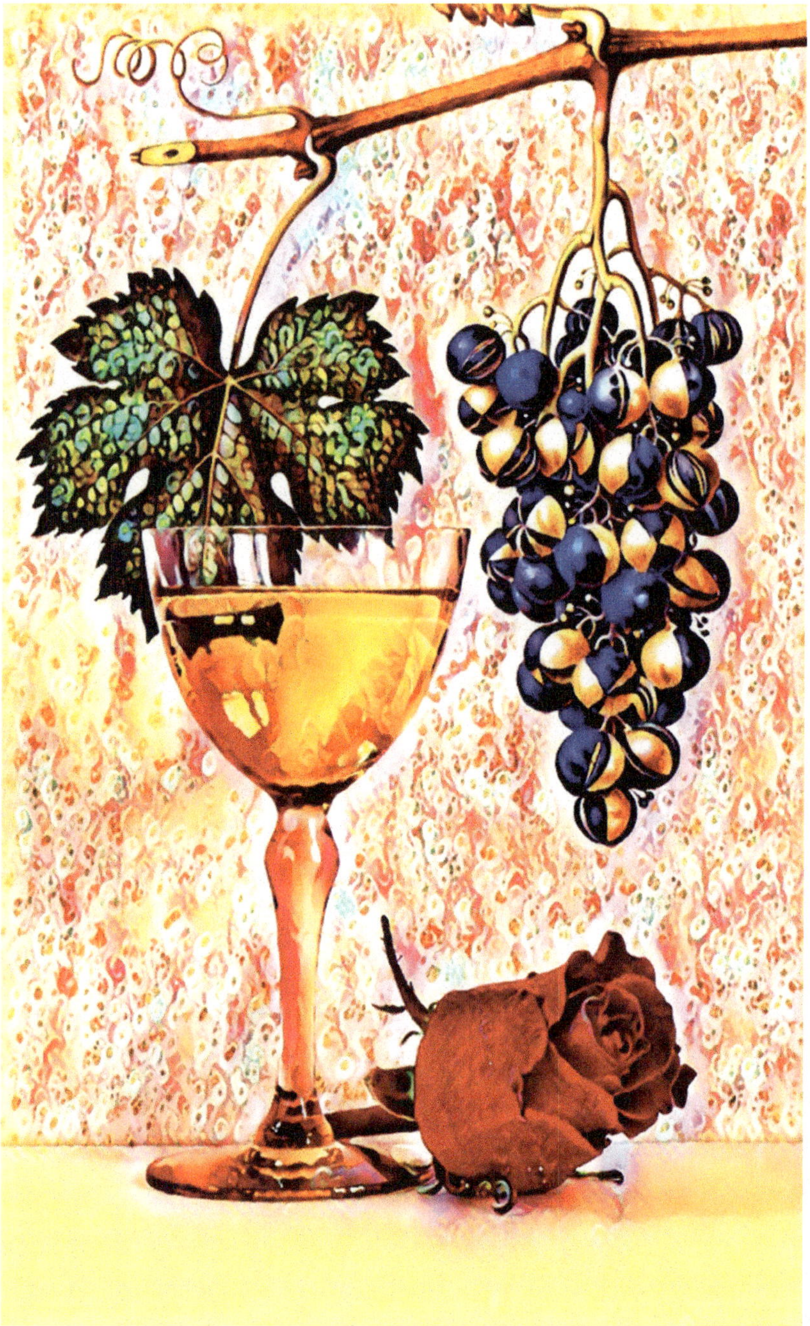

Bacchanalia

I wish I had a decadent Roman banquet in front of me, on which I could gorge, and fill myself with infinite sensations and pleasures.

It is a pleasant March night in the beautiful land of Tuscany, perfect time for one of my famous celebrations. The long rustic wooden tables are set exactly the way I imagined, scattered all over the magnificent gardens of Villa Bacchanalia, the numerous silver candelabras illuminating the plates, crystal and gold glasses. Grapes are flowing, white, red and black. The delicate wine decanters from Murano are already filled with strong nectars, drinks of the gods, ravishing promises of a sweet ecstasy. Loaves of bread of many forms, flavoured with olives, walnuts, rosemary and thyme are sitting next to a profusion of cured meats and cheeses, surrounded by fruits of all sorts.

The evening is deliciously warm and the full moon is spreading its scintillating rays, irradiating the scene. I can already hear the laughters of my arriving guests, having convivial conversations while they're walking through the enchanted gardens, admiring the decor set for this exceptional night. I can already feel the wine gently spinning their heads: women becoming more seductive, lascivious, laughing louder; and men becoming more affectionate, moving closer, getting drunk with the intoxicating perfumes on the temptresses' necks. With joy, I can perceive the hands touching, the obscene whispers in delicate ears. I can sense in my gut the inhibitions slowly disappearing, layer after layer.

Here we go. The night is young and yet there is this electric sexual tension in the air. What started as a dinner party will soon turn into an orgy under the power of my will. Each couple will forget about the world around them, too busy drowning in the sensual promise of a smile, a touch, a word. The energy is filling me as clothes fall to the ground, hands becoming more adventurous, from a shy contact to a sensual caress. Bodies and minds are heating up; kisses are exchanged. I am here, triumphant Bacchus, standing above them, king of the party, exciting partners, chanting mating incantations. It is unreal: my guests are in another dimension, embracing my cult, where there is no shame or taboo, but only the beauty of carnal pleasure.

Their desire is growing quickly — women are panting, aroused to the point they forget their chaste behaviour or position in society. They are my creatures now. Naked bodies are interlaced; beautiful moving paintings, sculptures of flesh embracing their deepest desires. There is no time, no place, no world. There is only here and now. The fumes of alcohol break the last reticence. The tongues become more passionate, intrusive, the hands more adventurous and the motions faster. Men finally conquer the last place, courageously diving into women's burning loins, filling them with their strength, their bestiality, their fantasies. Screams of pleasure are coming from everywhere, composing a strange but yet exhilarating melody. I, Bacchus, am dancing and singing on the table, empowered, admiring my Chef d'Oeuvre, proud of my ability to give back the human mind to Nature's needs.

Once again, I succeeded, untying the ropes of guilt usually constraining humankind, in the name of a god who never appears. I am here, right now, living among humans, sharing their hardship on earth. What kind of life would it be if we were to deny and refuse the sensual gratifications that Nature gives us?

I can hear the first orgasm, followed by many more, in total synchronicity: they reach the paroxysm, a holy communion in the religion of the senses. I, the liberator, am reinvigorated — my mission here is done. I am packing up, tiptoeing to the exit, leaving my guests to recuperate from the most intense night of their lives, emerging from the land of alcohol and sex. I am heading to my next destination, on the other side of the planet, where the sun is just setting, dusk appearing; I can set the scene for another decadent orgy and fill others' mind with my so-called perverted energy.

Opera

Life is like an opera, divided into several acts. Generally the beginning, the middle and the end, but we never know when the curtain drops. It always does, but when? When we are old, wise and with a happy sense of realisation, or when we are in total despair? Is it a tragedy or is it a comedy?

Life is like an opera, requiring so many musicians, dancers, technicians, a director and a maestro working together in order to create a beautiful symphony.

Life is like an opera, keeping the sorrow, the fights, the catastrophes and the hard work behind the scenes, only showing the gilt and the dreamy painted ceiling to the spectators.

Life is like an opera, with layers of different textures and tastes stacked on the top of each other: From the bitterness of the coffee to the smoothness of the buttercream, from the nourishment of the almonds to the sweet comfort of the chocolate, each flavour has its chance to shine and to complement the other ones.

My life is like my Opera Rock, beautiful, full of surprises around the corner, the crunchiness and lift of the hazelnuts, the punch of the alcohol, the added layer of chocolate to swirl my senses in a luscious dance; and I am the maestro.

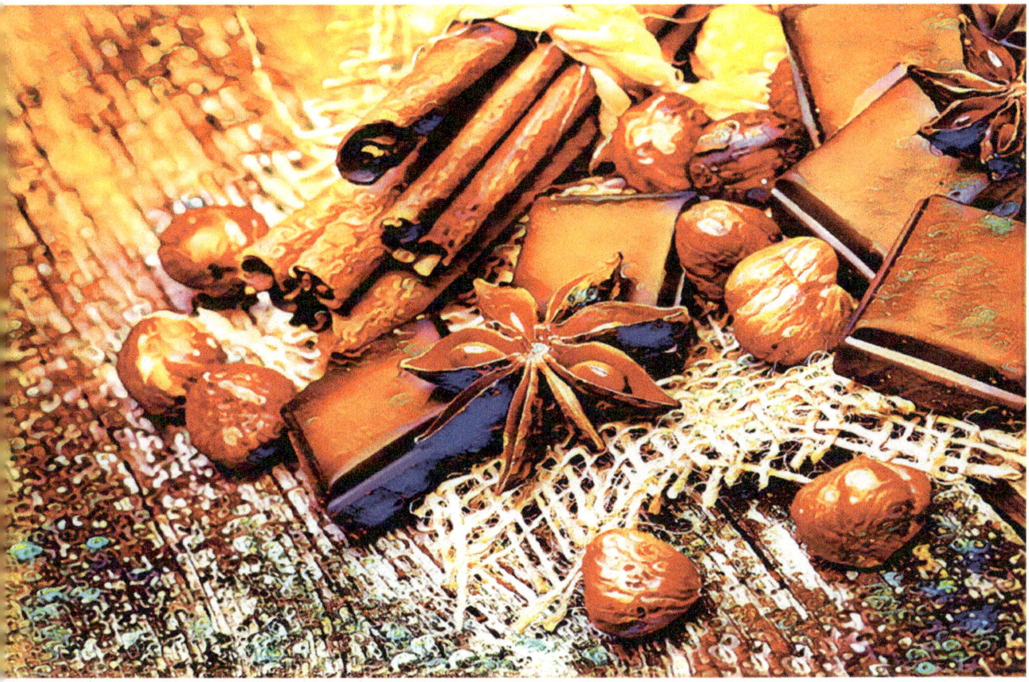

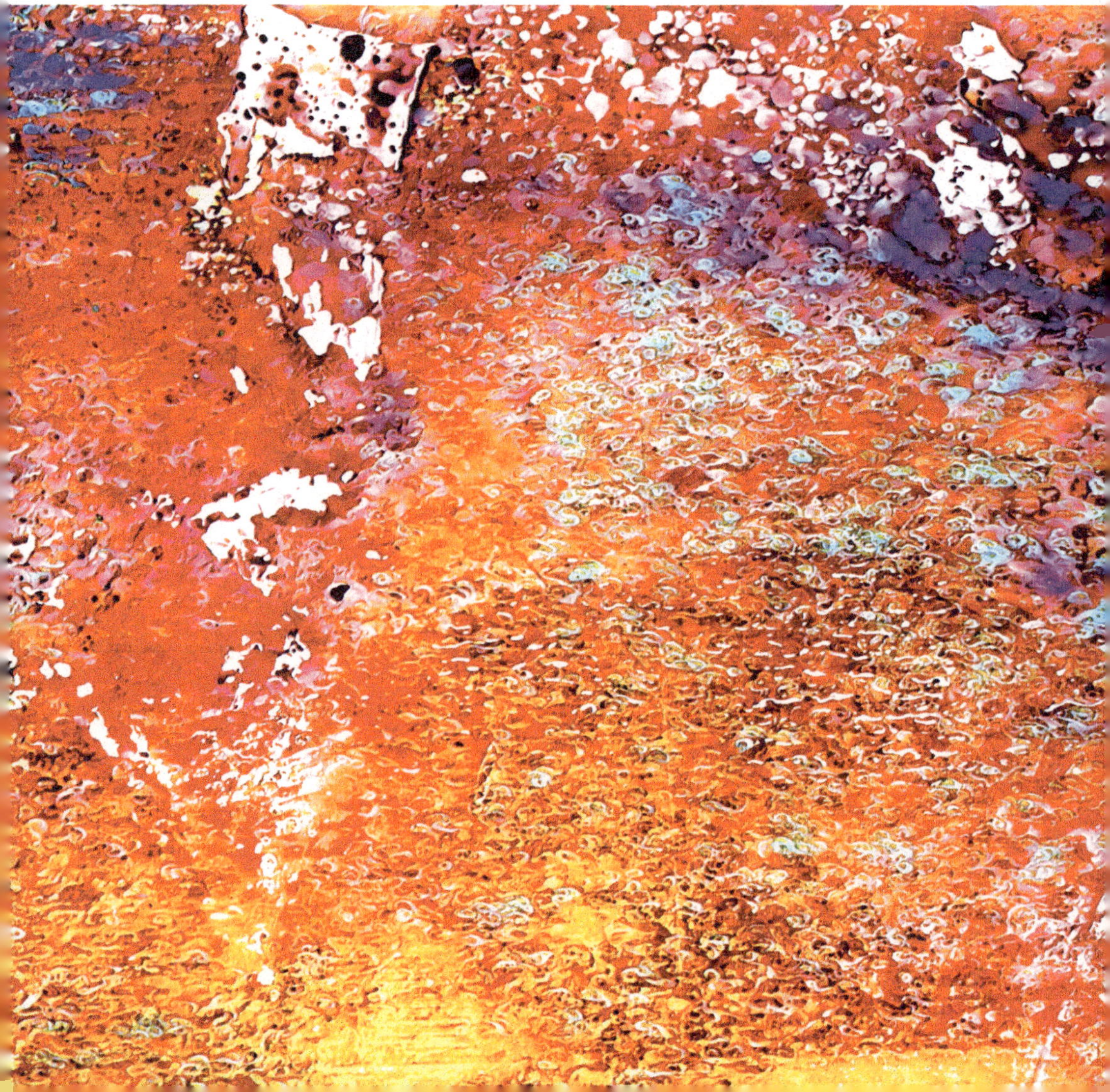

Aphrodisia

The Fallen Angel

He arrived by surprise, totally unexpected, tiptoeing behind my back until brushing against me. I recognised the mesmerising melody he was whispering in my ear. That wasn't the first time we met.

He was not that handsome — far from perfect in fact. He could be tyrannical, cruel sometimes, but his dark eyes were captivating, his smile charismatic, inviting me to trust him. Why would I assume he was any different from at our previous encounters?

Then he started singing louder, the same words over and over, a chorus I'd heard many times before. But his voice was deeper, deliciously fascinating. The lyrics became meaningful, hypnotising me. He faced me, pulled me against his chest, and a vibrant wave of his manly energy invaded me. He was holding my back in that way that meant: don't worry, I got you…His other hand, warm, strong, possessive even…on my neck: you are mine!

Yes, I was his…but not quite yet. My gaze on his forearm discerned a tattoo: FOREVER. My heart was beating in my ear. Panting but not scared, I was feeling his touch so soft, the comfort of his broad shoulders, the warmth of his breath caressing my face. Little by little my boundaries were disintegrating. The contact of his smooth lips on mine conquered me at last. That was it!

Forgotten the pain, the tears, the sorrow! Bewitched by his

scent, exquisite fragrance of musk and citrus, I was giving up, drowning in his mystical world, perfectly conscious that…that I was definitely surrendering to him…But this time it would be different, no? I will not be left destroyed and disenchanted by his domination.

He was more real than ever, authentic…so alive…Once again, I was diving into the arms of this Fallen Angel called Love.

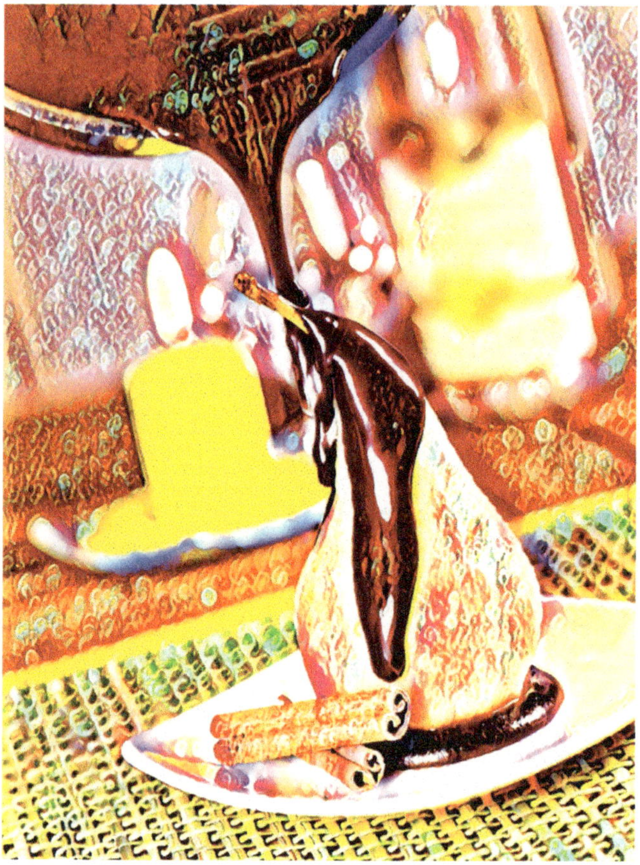

The Lover

Although she didn't value enough their relationship, it was simple: he was her best friend and her lover, always loyal, never a single question asked.

Sometimes she didn't look at him, turned her back on him, ignored his calls. She blamed him, despised him even…guilty of this shameful affair poisoning her mind, screaming evidence of her weakness, her neediness of his comforting presence in her life.

A love–hate story.

But she loved him dearly, passionately, adored him because he made her feel so good. After all, who did they think they were to judge her?

She closed her eyes, a burning desire consuming her. She caressed him slowly, immersed herself in his bittersweet scent, and finally abandoned herself. Her heartbeat was skyscrapering; she could feel this warm powerful wave emerging from her gut, intensifying more and more until she reached it. At the paroxysm of pleasure, an explosion of senses went through her entire body. His spicy flavour on her tongue, the warm smooth elixir of joy going down her throat, his sensuality enveloping her…delicate, intimate, never vulgar.

A peaceful satisfaction invaded her, carnally and emotionally. She was happy, fulfilled, revealed to herself by his touch.

God she loved Chocolate!

For One Mug of Solitary Pleasure

50 grams dark chocolate (at least 58 per cent)
150 millilitres hazelnut milk
Chantilly cream (recipe page 79)
1 teaspoon vanilla sugar
Dutch cacao

Over low heat, melt the hazelnut milk and the chocolate together. Stir until beautifully combined. Take off the heat, pour the luscious mixture into a pretty mug. Top it with a generous amount of chantilly cream and sprinkle with vanilla sugar and Dutch cacao.

Now you're all set for few minutes of ecstasy. Close your eyes and let the magic invade your senses.

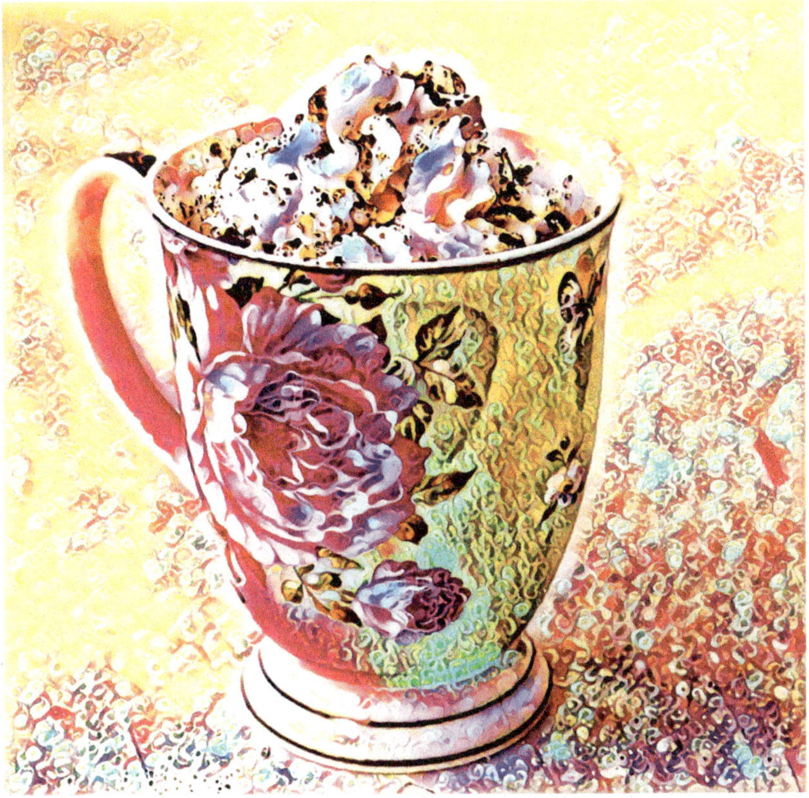

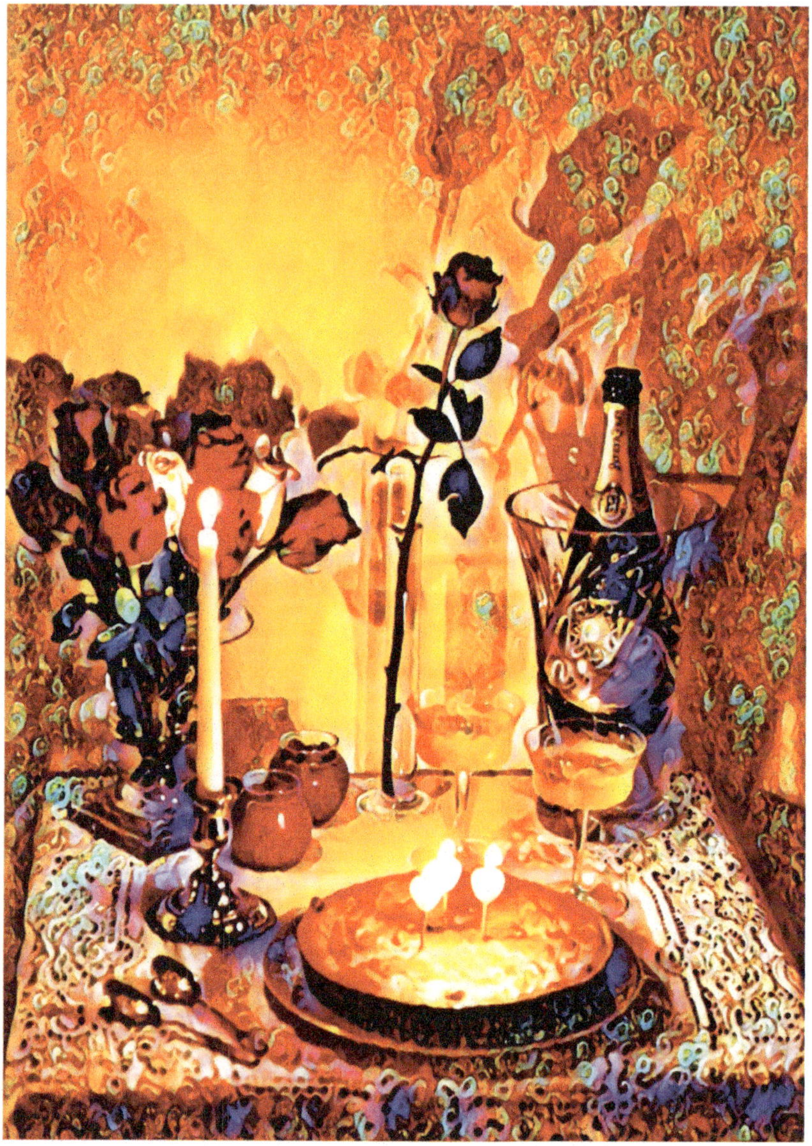

Romance

I put the white lace felt on the pedestal table strategically placed in front of the chimney, arranging the gold and blue china plates, the silver cutlery and the crystal glasses in an intimate setting. A tiny jar with a purple hydrangea and the precious vase, inherited from my grandmother, filled with ice, keeping the Champagne chilled, are complementing the decor. I put a candelabra on each side of the hearth, in the middle, a vase engraved with the word Amour, holding a bouquet of red, pink and white roses and peonies. I carefully light the fire and the candles, step back and admire the gorgeous presentation, promise of a romantic night.

    I go upstairs, sit in front of my portable Art Deco dressing table, which lies on an antique detailed wooden card table, and start the process of revealing my fatal beauty. With the aim of staying natural, I hide the signs of fatigue and stress with a little bit of concealer, and apply with a light brush on my face some expensive illuminating powder. To enhance my blue beryl eyes flecked with gold, I put some cream-coloured eye shadow on my lids and choose a copper-bronze one to emphasise the almond shape of my most attractive feature. I brush the blond tip of my eyelashes with dark brown mascara, revealing their length and curves; I domesticate my eyebrows in a sophisticated way, blush my cheekbones with terracotta powder, and coat my heart-shaped lips with scintillating aureate gloss.

Looking at myself in the mirror, I perceive the feline sensuality behind my angelic face. Dropping my robe, I look at my silhouette, admire my firm breasts, impressively sublime considering my age and the fact that they gloriously fed my daughter. My gaze goes down to my belly, a bit rounder that I wish, and my voluptuous hips, guardian of my femininity, inspiration of males' deepest desires, give me confidence in my sex appeal.

I take the Baccarat-designed bottle of Shalimar, enveloping my delicate skin with the scent of vanilla, tonka bean, jasmine and bergamot, oriental fragrance inspired by the Garden of Shalimar in Lahore, an expression of love from the Mughal Emperor Shah Jahan to his adored wife Mumtaz Mahal.

I dress my legs with a pair of black transparent tights, and don an elegant décolleté black lace dress, revealing gracefully my curves in a 1960s style. I delicately slip into my black velvet Prada heels, last touch but not the least to my beautification, shaping my feet, ankles and legs in a sexy way.

I tame my fauve mane, lustre my hair with argan oil, and then rush to the kitchen to prepare a luscious dinner for my lover.

I should start with dessert — something not too elaborate, not too fancy but yet decadent. Chocolate is the perfect ingredient. Chocolate mousse is the ultimate lovers' dessert. I take my Ecuadorian dark bittersweet, put it in a jug over a bain marie; while waiting for it to slowly melt, I separate the eggs, beat the whites with a pinch of salt until snowy soft peaks, and keep the yolks in a large bowl. Now the chocolate is deliciously shiny and smooth fluid, I pour it into the sunset-coloured yolks and mix them together frenetically until homogenised. I then put a third of the whites in the mix, folding them delicately, going up and down in a cautious circular motion, turning the bowl at the same time. And I add the rest, folding continuously, slowly, watching the mousse coming to life, light, airy. It deserves the most beautiful case as does a precious jewel. I take two crystal Champagne coupes from Murano, engraved with my initials, a gift for my eighteenth birthday. I have used them only twice since then, they are so fragile. But tonight is a special night. I pour the decadent chocolate mousse in them, and let the magic operate in the coolness of the fridge.

The doorbell rings. I look at myself once more in the mirror. Beautiful. My heart squeezes a bit as I open the door, and I melt in front of his loving smile. I am the one incurably charmed.

"Happy anniversary, my love" he whispers, grabs my waist and kisses me.

Lover's Chocolate Mousse

210 grams dark chocolate (at least 58 per cent)
6 eggs
1 pinch salt

Paris: A Romantic Fantasy

It's Sunday morning. I am still asleep, and very tired, as I worked very hard during the week, juggling my job, my kids and my man. A delicious scent is tickling my nostrils, slowly and gently waking me up. The bed is warm and cosy, and I am still full of reminiscences from my dreams. I don't know where I am any more — dozing, swimming between sleep and semi-consciousness, letting my imagination run back to the streets of Paris on a Sunday morning, where pedestrians are enchanted by the bewitching scent coming from the boulangeries.

Man after man is entering the bakery shop, buying croissants and chocolate croissants or other brioches for their wives, girlfriends or sweethearts. None of them planned this detour, but they couldn't help it. Every Sunday morning since the nineteenth century, a fragrant cloud falls over the city, waking up men, keeping women in a state of sleep. The men go out to the florist to buy beautiful bouquets for their ladyloves, then to the pastry shop. They go back to the apartment, prepare a beautiful tray, put a flower in a soliflore and the rest of the bouquet in a vase, place the still-warm viennoiseries on a plate, squeeze some oranges for a pulpy juice and prepare a favourite drink: tea, coffee or hot chocolate.

My man is even more dedicated. He browses through my recipe

notebook, finds the crêpes recipe an elderly Jewish woman from North Africa transmitted to me when I was seventeen, which is sensational because it doesn't need any resting time. It is simple, easy to make, light and delicious. So he puts 125 grams of flour in a bowl, then cracks three big eggs over it one by one, and mixes until combined. Then he adds half a tablespoon of sugar, two tablespoons of olive oil, because I like it like that, and my personal touch: a good lid full of fruity white rum. He mixes everything and then slowly pours while whisking with a fork, 250 millilitres of goat milk. He continues whisking until there are no lumps, heats a little bit of oil in a pan and makes a good pile of crêpes. He fills them with hazelnut spread or maple syrup and adds them to the tray.

He enters the bedroom, stays there for a minute, takes a few moment to look at the beautiful woman who shares his life, me, now moving in my sleep. He remembers why he fell in love with me, then delicately places the tray on the bed, kisses me softly and caresses my hair. I emerge from my sleep, fresh as a rose, smiling at my lover and my breakfast, deeply moved by his thoughtfulness, falling in love again. I kiss him, and then bite into a buttery croissant, while picking up a crêpe in my other hand.

This is my weekly moment when I relax, feel loved and satisfied in my gourmandise. I know that his day will be all about making me happy, making me feel as if I was the most beautiful and loved woman in the world, that I am singularly loved by him. Later on, we go for a walk holding hands on the Bords de Seine, and have a light lunch al fresco under the sun. We take in everything around us with loving eyes, feeling like we are the only ones in the world. Then, we go to the theatre, the opera or the movies, depending on our mood. We go back home tired, make love and fall asleep early in each other's arms.

On Monday mornings, the magic disappears, with the stress

of going back to work, the time spent commuting, grey Paris crowded with stressed people. Smiles fade, arguments rise, but every Sunday, Paris spreads its magical loving blanket over every couple's home all over again.

Ah, if only it was real…

Crêpes

125 grams flour
3 large eggs
250 millilitres goat milk
½ tablespoon caster sugar
2 tablespoons oil
1 lid of fruity white rum
Pinch of salt

I use goat milk because it's more digestible than cow milk, and it makes the crêpes lighter.

I also make my crêpes with extra virgin olive oil, but you can use unflavoured oil if you prefer.

Tango Argentino

The music starts. He is coming towards you, walking with that feline attitude, male grace's quintessence, almost hypnotising.

He takes your hand and brings you to the dance floor. Not a word, just his masculine self-confidence overwhelming all your senses.

The rhythm is beating in your head; you can feel the Latin lament invading you, taking possession of you…and you are gone for a journey in an exotic land.

With his body against yours, the temperature is rising. Don't surrender too fast, not yet. Offer some resistance or you won't be able to handle his strong hold. It is a joust of power, Querida.

Perceiving the warmth of his touch in your back, you start boiling: your cheeks are as red as tomatoes, sweat is slowly running down your spine and your breath is becoming shorter, jolting.

Don't let him control you. It is a Tango, a sexual duel. Invite him closer to better push him away. Make sensuality your best weapon, dominate him by commanding your senses: subjugate him. Otherwise he will leave you at the end of this musical incantation, conquered, blistered, water unable to relieve the fire consuming you.

Answer Chilli's mesmerising appeal only if you can triumph over him.

Chantilly Cream

The foam of the freshly whipped cream in the shiny copper bowl that has been in our family for decades brings back memories of when I was lying on this very table, the one on which my grandmother used to cook all our meals…with my pants down by my ankles and my lover drizzling Chantilly cream over my body to lick it straight back off. Delicately, starting from the back of my ear, travelling slowly to my shoulder blade, then sucking the unctuous, milky texture from my erect left nipple while his right hand firmly grabbed my bum. He next passed his tongue around my belly button, and a shiver shook me. The uncontrollable desire rising from my burning loins made me forget about the family dining in the living room, and I pushed his head down. I exhaled a gasp of relief when he started eating me voraciously, his fingers going deeper, claiming my body in such a way that my inhibitions disappeared like smoke in the wind. I jumped off the table, tore at his shirt, pulled off his pants, grasped his firm cock and swallowed it. My tongue made circular motions, and I could feel his heartbeat in my throat, my hands caressing his testicles, gently pressuring his sacrum. I licked him as if he were a gelato melting on a hot day, holding his penis firmly, masturbating him slowly, and then sucked his balls. He let a scream of pleasure escape and lifted me back onto the table. He flipped me over, strongly held my neck with one hand and penetrated me with force. I bit my lip not to scream, but whispered, "Fuck me hard, baby!"

Jolts became more vigorous, deeper, faster…his sweat ran down my back. I was on fire, about to faint; bliss grew from my vagina, taking entire possession of me, until the big shiver in my brain, where I lost consciousness of what was around me, aware only of both our bodies merged in one. He bit the back of my neck as he came inside me, and halting warm flows hosing my cave, satisfaction filling me.

A moment later, we switched back to reality, kissing each other, before rapidly getting dressed.

"Is the dessert coming any time soon?" asked Granny, opening the door.

We looked around and burst into laughter.

I whispered to my love: "Well, we'd better get an idea quickly, because there is no more cream for the Pavlova."

Now to prepare a luscious Crème Chantilly, which will make your lover want to eat you:

Pour 300 millilitres of rich whipping cream in a bowl. Choose a deliciously plump vanilla pod, and split it open lengthwise with a paring knife. Scrap the fragrant seeds out of her fertile belly, and incorporate them into the milky elixir. Add the pod. Cover the bowl with plastic wrap and let the exotic spices infuse in the coolness of the fridge overnight.

When the time has come and the vanilla has given her subtle yet sophisticated touch to the cream, remove the pod. Keep the mixture in a cold state — lay the bowl on a bed of ice if necessary.

Sweeten this promise of intense pleasure with 24 grams of the purest icing sugar. A little bit of this devilish ingredient always brings decadence to the scene.

Start whisking until the texture gets more body, becomes

rounder and forms waves. Don't beat the mixture too long or it will escape you. When taking out the whisk, a scrumptious curl should appear and the waves hold in a beautiful pattern.

Crème Chantilly

300 millilitres whipping cream (at least 30–35 per cent fat)
24 grams pure icing sugar
1 vanilla bean

A Man Cooking For You

How sexy is a man cooking for you?! He told you to put your feet up, relax and enjoy a glass of wine, and now he is moving around the kitchen gathering ingredients and utensils.

While you're sipping an expensive French nectar, you notice his prominent muscles when he's chopping the vegetables, the concentration on his face. Or should I say the dedication, because he's on a march, with the ultimate aim of pleasing you.

While looking at him, you are seeing him for the first time. You have the leisure to observe every centimetre of his body without your gaze bothering him. He is so absorbed in his task that he doesn't even realise you are drinking him, not the wine.

Your eyes are wandering from his forehead to the curve of his plump lips, from his broad shoulders to his strong large capable hands; you're leering at him, and fantasising already about dessert when the meal is not even ready. He is your appetiser, the one you are craving. You're not hungry for food any more.

At this very moment, he's showing you his love in a stronger way than with words or promises. Therefore you have to wait patiently. You must silence your desire, tame it and let it slowly grow. Imagine it's your first date, and seduce him all over again. Then all what he will want is to keep pleasuring you all night long.

Insert here the perfect meal
a lover, man or woman,
would cook for you.

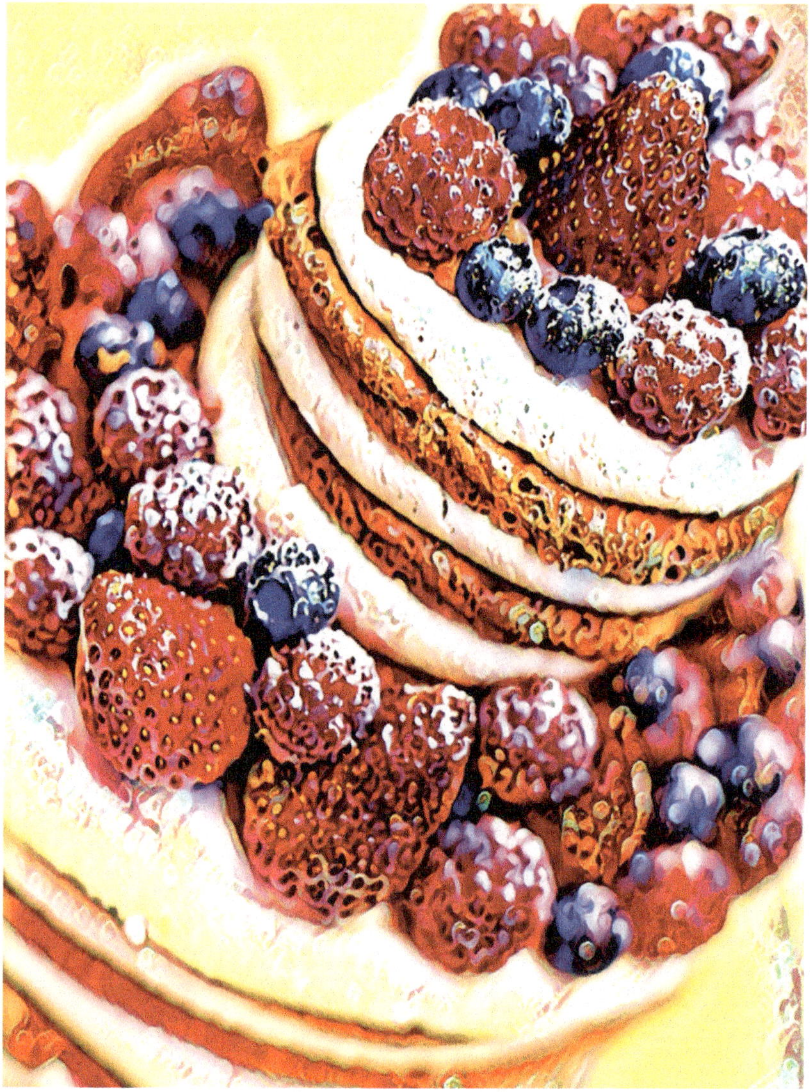

Desire

I am burning with desire, anticipating unknown pleasures, letting my imagination fill itself with decadent fantasies, already grieving at the unbearable thought that it won't last forever.

My lips are slightly opening, waiting for his delicate kiss. I am drooling at the idea of devouring him. I slowly pull him towards me, until he has no other choice than to surrender to my insatiable lust. Our bodies unite in a delicious fusion. I am feeding on him, impregnating myself with his sweetness, enjoying each of our ephemeral kisses, opening myself to a violent ecstasy, an explosion of senses. He disappears, leaving me alone. My will weakens, already addicted to the rush of warm happiness he brought to my heart. Let's take a second bite of this scrumptious Cake.

Lady Velvet

As summertime approaches and the temperature rises, I can already discern the delicate curves of her body and her velvety skin. I dream of the refreshing taste of her succulent flesh, sweet nectar dripping down my throat as I suck her exquisite juices.

It is not time yet. She is too young, too shy to endure my caresses. She has to mature, soften to the idea that I am going to take delight of her one of these days, waiting for her cheeks to blush under my libidinous glance. I am incapable of hiding my shameful thoughts, drooling in front of her perfect silhouette, promises of divine pleasures. I am thirsty for her incredible life to touch me, her roundness to tease me. My desire is at its peak and I am desperate to kiss her. I fantasise about savagely biting into her delicious pulp. It is too much to bear — I won't have the patience to slowly undress her — I will just make her mine, indecently burying my nose into her flavoursome parts, ripping off a large bite out that Peach like the wild animal I am.

You can make a delicious variation of the clafoutis, using peaches or nectarines instead of cherries.

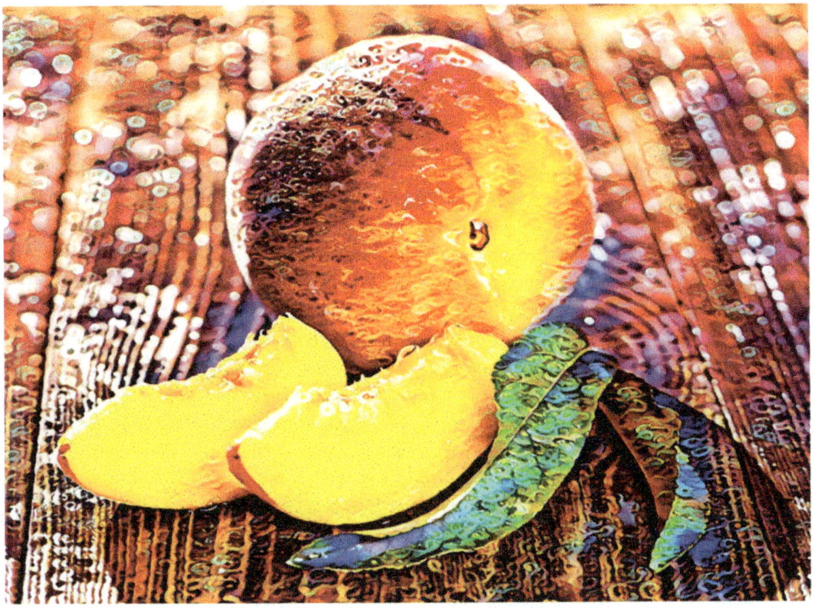

Jealousy

I want to say I have no idea who he's talking about, but we both know that would be a lie. I can see the sparkle in his eyes, the lust, everything in his behaviour showing that he has fallen hard for her. I am envious, jealous not to be able to trigger such a burning desire in my lover's heart and body any longer. I feel dull, ordinary, faded by her brightness and his need of her. Now he barely looks at me, instead he drools for her curves, her bubbles. She poisons his mind, runs through his veins like cocaine.

Why is it she who gives him relief? I know he's talking about her, I know he misses her, dreams about her, and it hurts me.

I am the jealous type. That is, until he introduced me to her brunette sister. At first, I didn't want to look at her, but at least she had a little bit more personality. She sent me obvious signals and waited for me. I resisted. But soon I surrendered, right in front of him. I couldn't help myself. I let her kiss me, and the most amazing feeling invaded my body when our lips touched. I felt relieved of a thirst which teased me and I hadn't known even existed. I started seeing her behind his back, addicted to her taste, at night, in secrecy first, then in the middle of the day, exposed to everyone's look. Soon it became a threesome, involving swinging couples too. She was so exciting, but even though I enjoy her company, I will always choose him in the end. But I do know the blonde is ruling his heart, making me an accessory he's proud to show off, a trophy. His love for me is not steady. His need of her is scary. He discards me to spend weekends alone with her, calling her sexy, his real true love, or the one who never lets him down. Their relationship is unhealthy. I tried to warn him several times of her dangerous hold on him, but he ended up resenting me even more.

It is very hard for me to compete, as she is everywhere, all the time, calling him.

I know I am not the only abandoned one. Many of you suffer too! Our men are obsessed with that sexy beer.

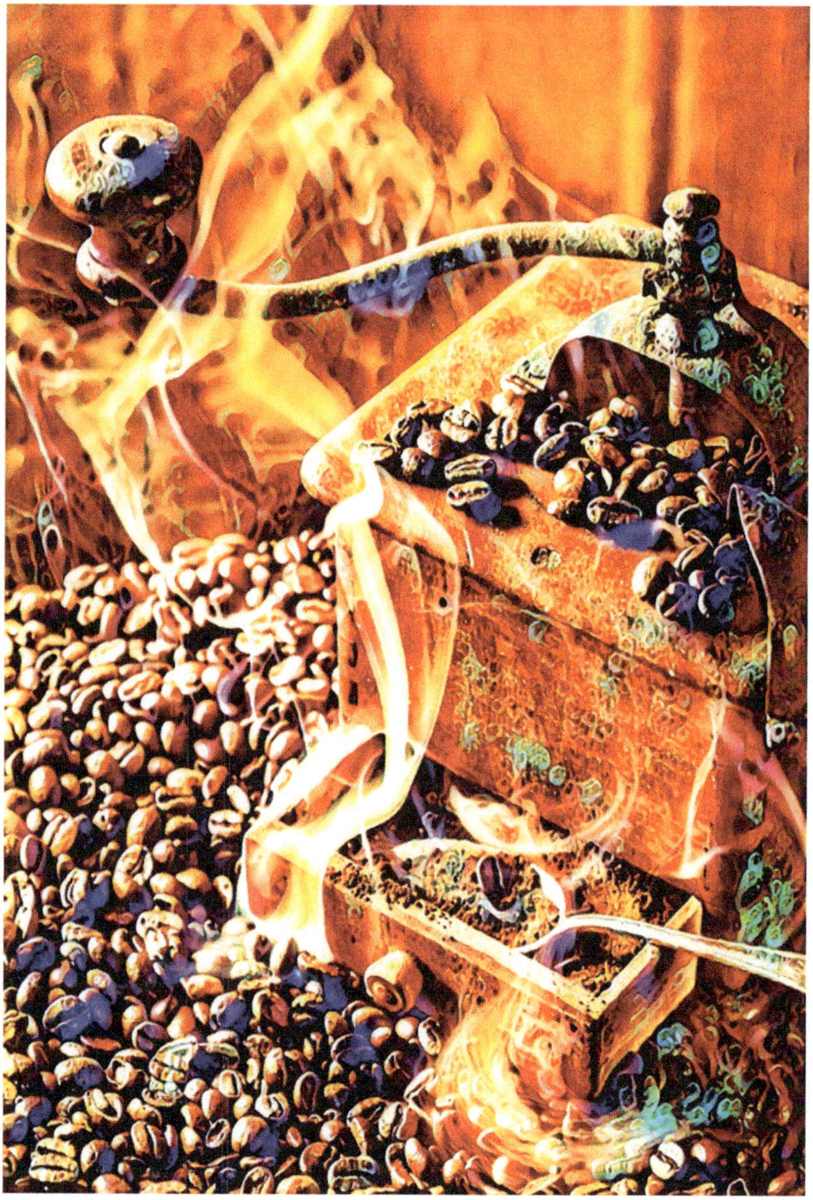

Sweet Poison

I am a risk taker, willing to live life at one hundred per cent. Every morning, I throw myself at your neck, diving into the turmoil of our intense love story, falling in love with you all over again, day after day, despite the sleepless and anxious nights our relationship is causing me. Every morning, I feel this warm wave growing inside of me, forgiving and forgetting the palpitations, the cravings. I know you're not good for me, that you're going to put me on an emotional roller coaster, but I can't help it. I need this rush of adrenaline making me feel so alive. I need to smell you, feel you, touch you, taste you. I am closing my eyes and fantasising about your scent and your velvety skin. I think about you constantly, as soon as I open my eyes in the morning, until I close them in the evening, already dreaming about our next encounter. You, exquisite evil, are haunting my nights, insidiously putting doubt into my mind, seeds of love and destruction.

How many times have I been told not to go back to you? How many times did I, on the edge, rush into your comforting arms? You are the one making me feel so awakened to life; you are my inspiration, my muse, my addiction. Without you I can't think clearly. Drinking life out of you, gorging on your energy, to fill the emptiness of my soul, I can finally find peace and clarity of mind as soon as I take the first sip of you, my beloved Coffee.

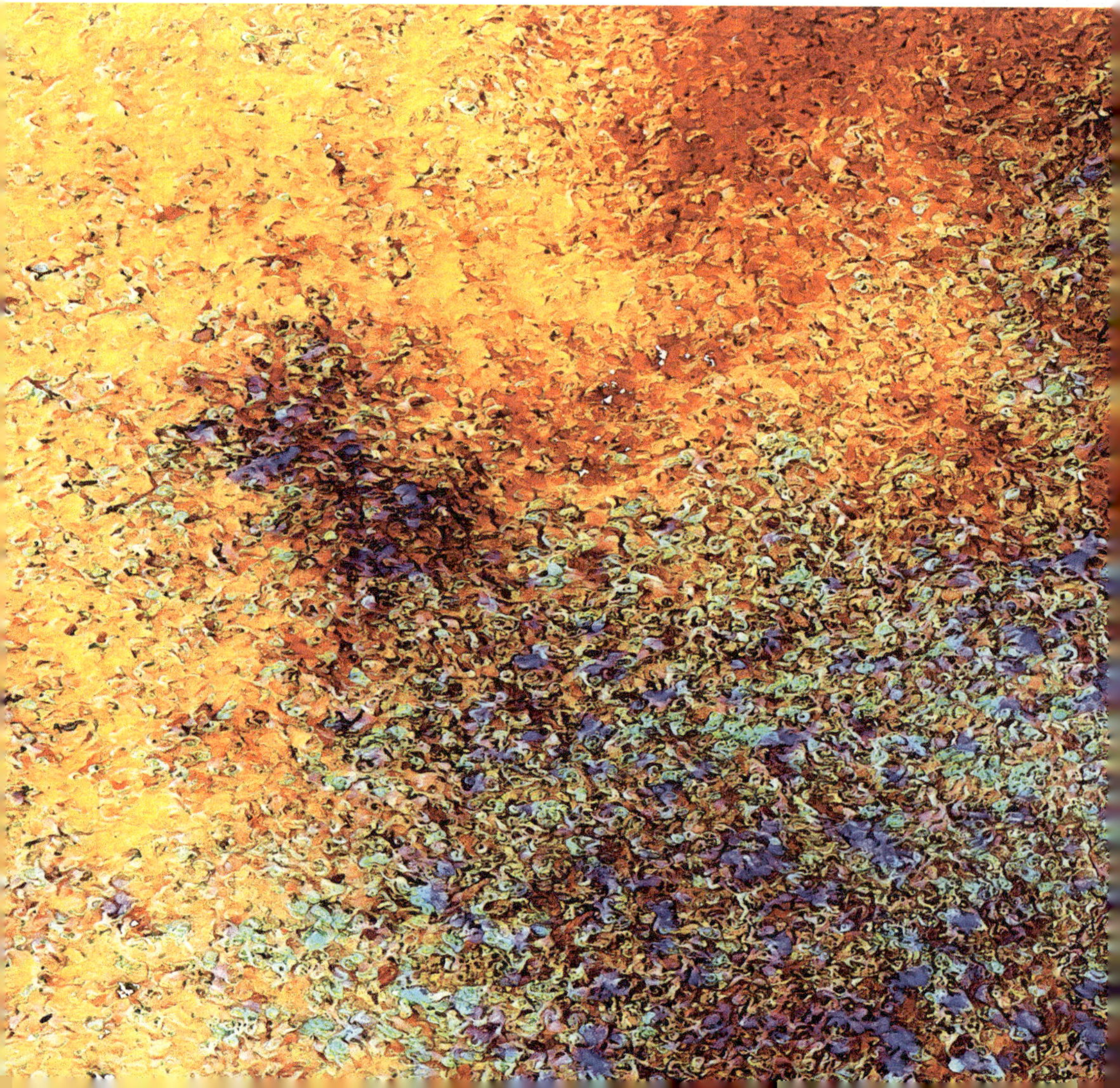

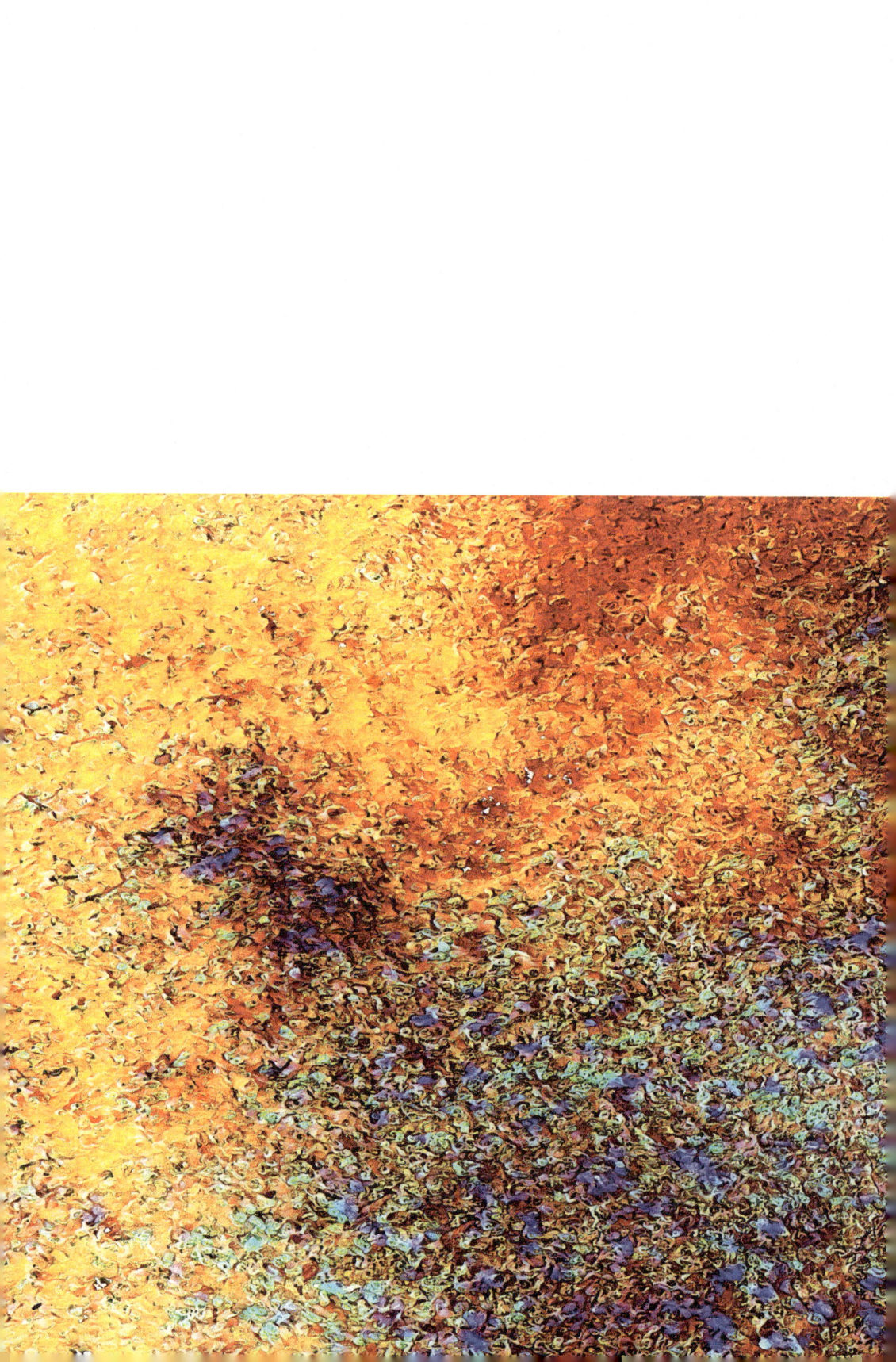

Exoticism

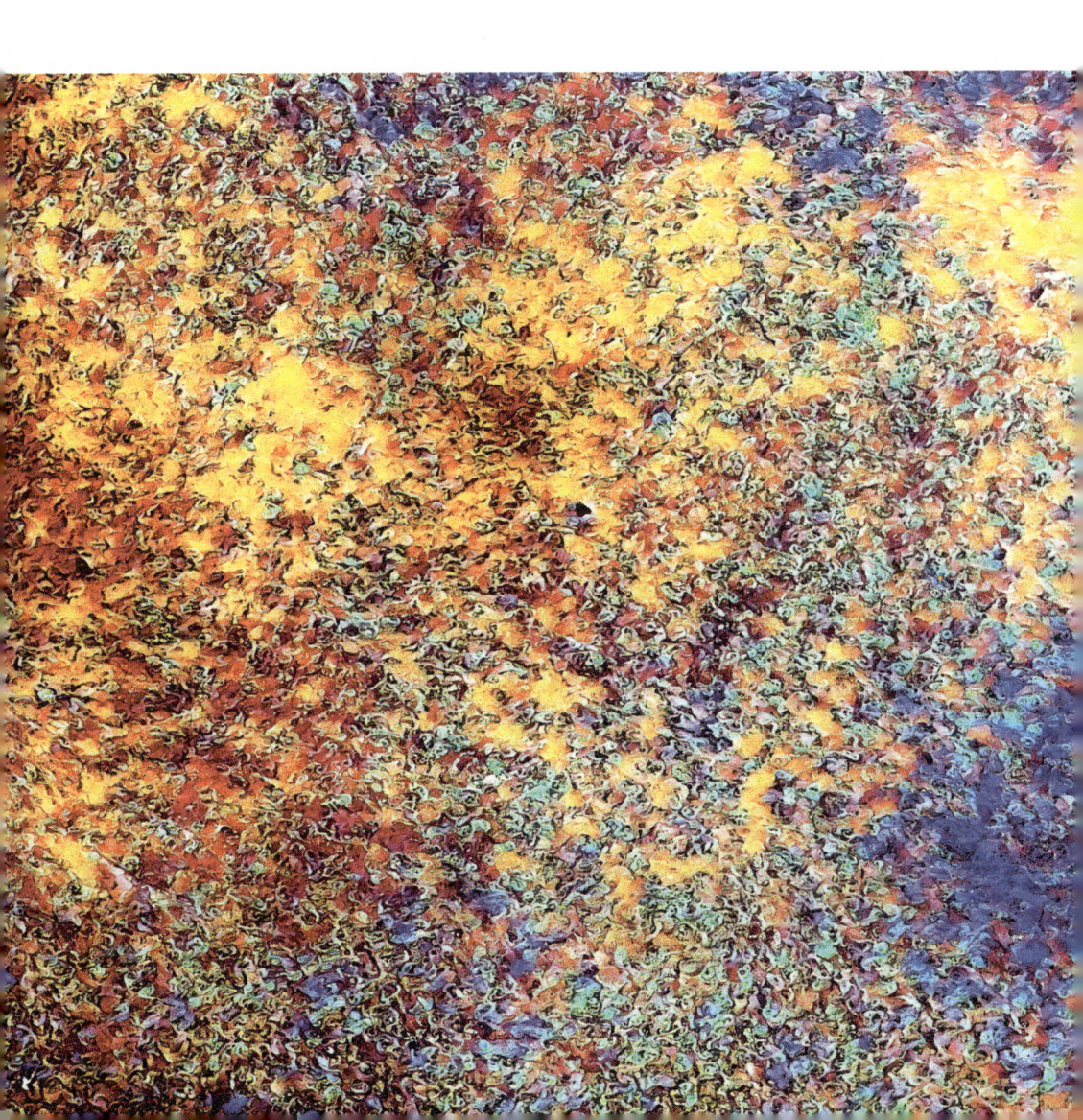

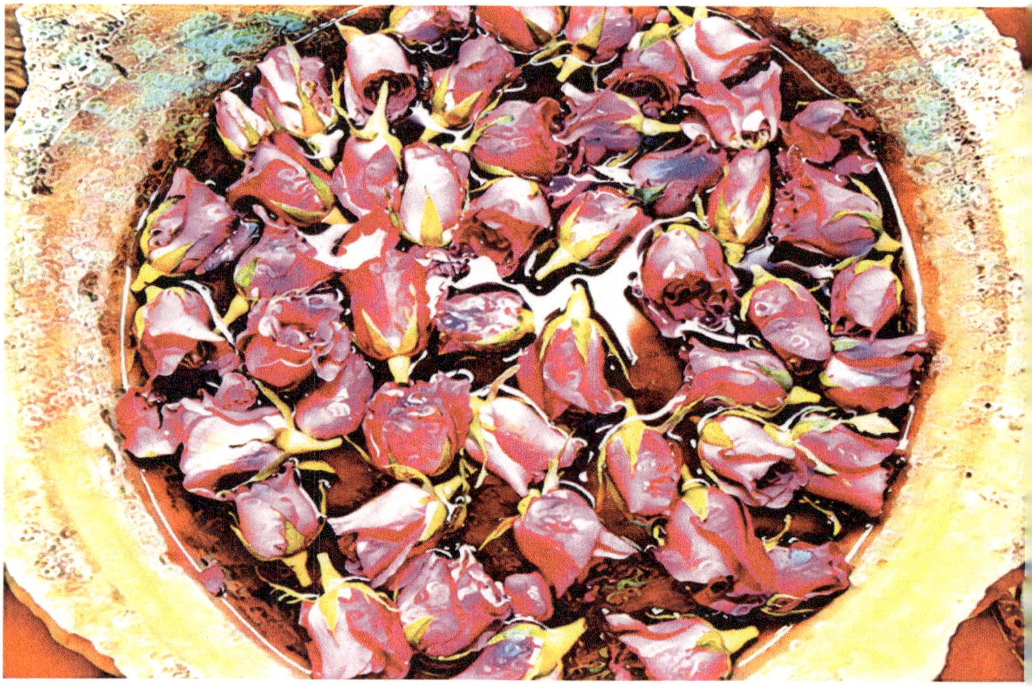

Bosphorus

I am drunk on her overpowering smell, my head spinning with reminiscent memories of oriental travels, secret gardens of which she is the Queen. She haunts my dreams, her delicate figure blossoming under the sun's caress, her soft skin irresistibly attractive. Where did we meet? On the tides of the Bosphorus, where she was gloriously illuminating the Sultan's patio; or in the coolness and sophistication of a European court? When did we meet? Last night, last year, last century, at the beginning of time? She has this universal and eternal beauty, incessantly calling men to court her, punishing them with cold blood if they don't surrender to her changing temper. Her obsessive fragrance triggers impossible dreams, and the addictive but subtle taste on my lips transports me to forgotten countries yet to be discovered. All I want is to build her sumptuous palaces, honouring her with gold and fine architecture. I want to tame her, own her, lock her in a gilded cage delicately chiselled, so the world could admire her perfection without profaning her. I want to gently extract all her emotions, shades, desires, aspirations and make them mine. I want the enchantment to be endless, timeless, borderless; but she slips through my fingers, withering as soon as I catch her, appearing only when it pleases her. O Rose, cruel magician, divine mistress, why did you set your heart on me?

Garden of Roses

In the ruins of Kandahar, magical city destroyed by hatred and war, remains the memory of an ancient glory. The relics of the oriental cradle of civilisation seep from the soil, too long watered with blood. The greed of humans, in their quest to own her, resulted in abuse of her, violation, leaving her exhausted and lifeless. Late at night, though, the breeze appeases with her cool caress; the minds heated by the burning sun, are haunted by reminiscences of her majesty. They dream of flamboyant gardens heavy with flowers and fruits, of a realm described in old tales, where populations from all around the world were living together, trading the most precious treasures in a joyful abundance of fragrances, spices, silks, silver and gold.

When Gulshan takes her veil off in the privacy of her home, she sometimes creates a sweet reminder of a time she never lived, when life and women's beauty was celebrated in a turbulence of senses. She starts with the essence of the dessert: some pieces of candied ginger and oranges she carefully keeps in a jar, rinsed, dried and finely chopped. She then heats some cream from the neighbour's cow, traded for some laundry work. Once the liquid is almost boiling, she pours it little by little on some white chocolate from the black market. She stirs well and then adds drops of rose water and orange blossom water she distils on her little patio, a secret piece of paradise she jealously keeps for herself, hidden from the community. Lastly she adds the small pieces of confit fruits, combines everything together and lets the smooth, heavenly scented mixture to cool in the freshness of the night.

In a larger bowl, she whisks creamy butter and sugar until they become one, then adds two eggs one by one, still whisking. She pours in a certain amount of flour so the mix will turn into a thick batter, and a pinch of salt, and, lastly, she folds in the luscious ganache. She pours the whole in a cake pan she has previously greased and puts it in the oven.

After few minutes, her entire house is filled with an enchanting smell, awakening her senses and her appetite. Her spirit is already escaping the hardship of Afghan reality. When Gulshan takes the cake out of the oven, its golden crust is so appealing she can't resist cutting a slice straight away. She closes her eyes before delicately putting a first piece in her mouth, already anticipating pleasure. As soon as the warm moist crumb touches her tongue, she is back in the golden times of Kandahar. Her imagination travels to the luxuriance of the Persian Empire, intoxicated by the rose and orange blossom aromas. She's revealed to herself, dreaming of performing a seven veils dance surrounded by thousands of flowers, millions of petals raining all over her. The sun is captivated by her alluring freedom. She has found her quintessence, the true meaning of her being, of her name, Gulshan. She is a garden of roses.

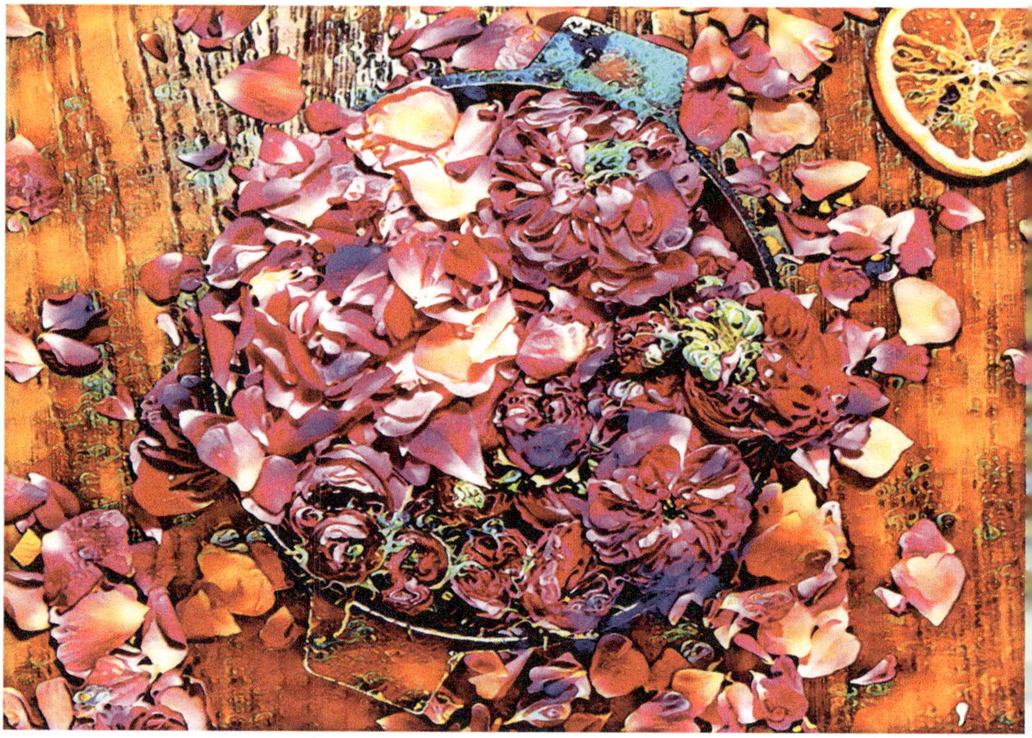

Kandahar Cake

ORANGE BLOSSOM/ROSE GANACHE
70 millilitres whipping cream
90 grams white couverture chocolate
6 grams orange blossom water
3 grams rose water
5 grams confit pomelos or oranges
5 grams ginger confit

CAKE
100 grams unsalted butter
100 grams caster sugar
2 large eggs
½ teaspoon vanilla extract or 1 vanilla bean
150 grams flour
Ganache
Pinch salt

Josephine Baker

After only two months in the big city, Josephine decided to become an exotic dancer. After all, her skin colour was exotic. Little she knew that she would have to dance half naked in front of an audience comprised of libidinous men and jealous women. She had to do something different to get on the top of the crowd: she didn't want to be seen as an easy girl but as an artist. Thinking about her childhood in tropical lands, she started dreaming about the islanders' outfits made out of straw and colourful hats. The fruit basket on the table caught her attention, nothing very fancy nor exotic, but what if she used fruits from the paradise: bananas, pineapples, pomegranates? What if she wore a skirt of bananas? Fresh bananas would make it impossible and be very expensive in the long run, but what if she made fake ones? Bananas would move along with her hips' motions, giving this little phallic subliminal idea and making her irresistible.

And so she did.

Her only defence was to write down every word they said. A negro half naked! Scandalous! Shocking! Despite this, the public kept on showing up, night after night, money kept on filling the till, and she was suddenly exposed to the whole country as a public figure. Better to be shamed, known but paid, than starving, cleaning the shit of others.

Journalists started to want to interview her. She told them she was the descendant of an African king, her great-grandmother was abducted from their land and sent to the West Indies as a slave. But everyone recognised she was a queen, and even the master of the house fell under her spell and worshipped her, giving her whatever she wanted and treating her like a queen, better than his own wife.

"There you go, making up lies again," her impresario said.

"What do you want me to say? That I come from the gutter of the city? We have to make them dream — they wouldn't pay to see some unknown black girl dancing, but they are to see an African queen."

"Very well, do as you wish!"

"They can't verify anyway; there is no genealogy in slaves' records," she reasoned.

And at each interview she added more details to her fairy tale story. The majestic lions tamed by her people, the freedom in the bush, the love story between her great-grandmother and the marquis. All with such precision, she described the immensity, the smells, the sun, the heat, the emotions, so that after a few months she was known as the Caribbean Queen. Men began to send her flowers, jewels, begging her to become their mistress. But she kept them at distance, teasing their appetite, staying inaccessible, so their desire would never die.

After New York she was called to Paris. Paris, the romantic city, land of literature, sophistication, artists. How excited she was.

Parisians were curious. Firstly their attention was caught by the sound of her naked feet when dancing, hitting the floor in a voodoo rhythm, then they would admire her sculptural body, her long brown legs, her round and firm bottom, moving sensually, an invitation to lust, their gaze would go up to her waist and then to her voluptuous breasts, moving with the music. They were hypnotised by such a display of flesh, without any shame, glorifying woman's body in all its splendour. They all loved her exoticism, her bright smile, her passion, her fire; they all lusted for her, men and women, dreaming of biting a little bit of this sweet paradise.

Josephine was living the high life, being the life of Parisian Parties, drinking Champagne and socialising with the high society and artists. She didn't have much time by herself and sometimes longed for the islander life she had invented. So when she was alone in her apartment, which was rare, she would take off her designer clothes, don a more comfortable outfit and put an apron on. She would then dismiss the maid and enjoy the solitude of her kitchen, and bake a sweet reminder of life in a plantation.

As the banana queen, she always had some shipped to her from Fort de France, capital of Martinique. She'd start by greasing a mould with butter, then mash two bananas, put flour, baking powder and salt in a bowl, cream some butter and raw sugar cane and add to it one egg, the banana mash and dry ingredients, and finally she would add a good lid of white rum to flavour the batter and give it some lift. She'd put the mix in the tin and bake it for around 35 minutes at 180 degrees Celsius.

While the base was baking, she would peel and slice five bananas, drizzle them with lime or lemon juice, according to what she had in the kitchen that day, and set them aside. Once the cake was ready and had this golden colour reminiscent of the warm sun, she'd put around two thirds of the sliced bananas in a pan, where she had previously melted a bit of butter and sugar. She would let the bananas caramelise while placing the other third on the top of the cake. Once the bananas were beautifully caramelised and sweetened she'd put them on the centre of the cake. She would finally sit, but not before having prepared a cup of luscious hot chocolate. In the middle of the night, Josephine

Baker wasn't any more the égérie of Paris but little Josephine from Saint Louis, indulging in all the deliciousness of warmer countries. She'd have a sip of chocolate then a bite of cake. All the Caribbean was wrapped into these two little treats, warming up her lonely heart that was tired by the noise of fame and misunderstood by individuals. Struggling to find real love, she sought comfort in her own dreams.

Josephine Baker Cake

125 grams flour plus some for the pan
80 grams soft butter plus some for the pan
Large teaspoon of baking powder
100 grams raw sugar
1 large egg
2 large ripe bananas
1 lid fruity white rum
Pinch of salt
4 bananas
1 lemon
1 lime
50 grams raw sugar
50 grams unsalted butter

Tropical Beauty

I want to beat you, smash you, shake you, cut you open so I can gorge on you, be regaled by the infinite variations of your being. Why are you so cruel to me when all I ask is that you to open to me? Reveal to me your secrets, all of them. What do you hide behind this hard shield you built to protect yourself from us? You are constantly teasing me, exciting my imagination with your perfect round bottom turned towards the sun as an offering. You don't make it easy for me to catch you, when all I want is to be by your side, silently watching the back and forth of the ocean, far away from civilisation, letting myself being slowly intoxicated by your scent. You climb higher and higher, out of reach, keeping our thirst for you always alive. I dream of your fragrance left on my skin after a night of passionate love, perfect tropical honeymoon spent walking on the beach, the shade of the palm trees in the glorious sunset, the hot sand under our feet. Ideal image of Heaven. You are the Paradise I am looking for, all the desert islands of the world would be dull without your presence. I dream of drinking water out of your lips, milk out of your breasts. I dream to bite into your soft porcelain flesh, and fall asleep in your arms. I dream of keeping you forever, bottling your exotic essence so I can perfume my gloomy winter days with your presence, inviting me to escape the boredom of life. I dream of your soft caress on my skin, smooth, aerial and sensual. I think about you all the time. I travelled so far to see you again, crossed many seas, worked all year round so I could take you out, invite you for drinks, dinner and maybe breakfast. Please my sweet little Coconut, open yourself so I can start my holidays with the mesmerising taste of you.

Caribbean King

He has always been a big part of my life. I feel lost without him. Like a dream catcher, he makes me feel safe, brings me to exotic destinations and adds excitement to whatever could be dull without his touch. There is something missing when he is not here, something indescribable, a subtle melancholia of what could have been.

Although he is strong, he knows how to bring refinement and elegance into the ordinary, how to break the monotony. From breakfast to dinner, he has this way of waving an invisible magic wand, enhancing what could be mediocre to the surprising exquisite.

Of course you don't realise how life changing he is if you haven't met him yet. But when you do, and you will, there is no way back. You won't appreciate your crêpes any more, nor your vanilla éclairs, nor your chocolate truffles: everything will taste banal, insipid sometimes.

He is this magician who brings your cuisine to the extraordinary, making you travelling to the Caribbean just by biting into a crème pâtissière, bringing this je ne sais quoi to your crêpes, waffles, banana bread, and subliming your decadent chocolate desserts.

I love his dark colour, his distinction, his warmth, his

roundness, his woody and spicy aromas. But I have to impregnate him with my personality too, to make him even better. So I add one or two vanilla pods to infuse in this delightful elixir for several months, and then the enchantment occurs, pure alchemy. Have you guessed his name yet? He is this wonderful spirit called Rum.

Vanilla Rum

1 bottle dark rum
2 vanilla beans

Carribbean Rice Pudding

5 handfuls Arborio rice
1 can coconut milk
1 glass water
2 tablespoons raw sugar
2 lids of vanilla rum

In a saucepan, pour one can of coconut milk and its equivalent of water. Split a vanilla bean lengthwise with a paring knife, scrape out the grains and put them into the liquid as well as the bean itself. Put on medium heat, add around five handfuls of Arborio rice, stir, and let it simmer for a while. Add another glass of water as the rice starts absorbing the liquid. When the rice is cooked, add two to three tablespoons of raw sugar according to your taste, and finish with two lids of dark vanilla rum. Serve while it's warm to enjoy all its exotic flavours.

Seraglio

She is holding the list of her rivals in her shaking hands, paired with their preferred method of murder. Most of them opt for poison, which is a typical way to get rid of a freshly arrived young beauty. This is why Nashkidil's slave tastes all her food, even though she now has the private kitchen earned by her elevated rank in the seraglio.

Sineperver is the most vicious of the rivals; she has many spies and can get anyone murdered by various methods — acid in massage oils, strangulation behind the fountains in patios, arsenic in incense or candles…

Nashkidil has to keep an eye on her if she wants to rule over the harem without fearing for her life. But first, she has to seduce the new padishah to keep her position, put her son on the throne when it's time and become the sultana valide, the most powerful woman of the Ottoman Empire.

Dusk is falling on Topkapi's gardens, illuminating Saint Sophia's dome of a scintillating blue aura. From her window, she can hear the evening prayer calling. She made up her mind: Selim will be hers — whatever it costs, the voodoo prophecy will happen. Desirée should know what to do, the charms, the potions, the incantations…she is a Caribbean witch's niece after all! There is not much time; tomorrow Selim is coming to visit her son

Mahmud, and will decide whether to send her to the old seraglio with all the former sultan's wives...or not.

She survived the sinking, the abduction, the slave market, the rivalries and the plots. She was initiated to the art of manipulation at the age of fourteen, otherwise she would be long time dead, buried and forgotten.

"Think, Nashkidil! Think!"

She remembers the almond biscuits she had in Nantes, when she visited her aunt before being sent to the convent. It is wise to add some freshness and Middle Eastern flavours to them, a perfect combination between Orient and Occident. Selim will not suspect anything as she will be eating them too: his inclination for sweets will do the rest.

Nashkidil rushes to the kitchen. The seraglio is asleep and silent. Desirée has already gathered the ingredients and is disposing the red candles for the ritual: a miniature painting of Selim and one of her mistress; and sandalwood incense. The kadine is chanting the love spell words until dawn, while confectioning the perfectly rounded petits fours, putting all her will into it. This is her only hope, her last chance.

The muezzin's voice reminds her to go back to her room before the hundreds of noisy shallow women animate the place with their constant chattering. She lies down on the scarlet and gold sofa and falls into a deep lethargy. Her black slave gently wakes her up, as it is time to get ready for the meeting with the sultan.

Nashkidil goes through all the beautification stages: hamman, cold shower, and aromatic oil massage under the strong expert hands of a German matron. She then envelops her body with a captivating scent, applies just a small amount of kohl on her eyes, leaves her abundant hair falling down her back and slips into a muslin robe that reveals her beautiful figure. She contemplates herself in the mirror: she looks perfect, deliciously attractive as if she were just rising from bed, mastering the subtle art of seduction. She spreads a few chiselled silver plates filled with the scrumptious delicacies all around her apartment and waits.

When, a few minutes later, Selim enters the room, Nashkidil is reading a book while flippantly nibbling on some strange petits gâteaux. He is impressed by her apparent calm, knowing that at this crucial moment, he could destroy her existence. She looks up at him, smiles, and gently invites him to share morning tea with her. The conversation starts with banalities, then moves to condolences, her husband the sultan was a good man. The new padishah feeling at ease, starts talking about his passion, Europe, and especially France, where she is from. He asks her about the little biscuits she is eating, and she shares with him childhood memories, and how she improved this regional culinary speciality to bring them to oriental decadency.

Selim takes one and bites into it — it melts in his mouth, it is delicate, crispy and moist at the same time, so sensual…He closes his eyes, letting the aromas infuse his mind, and imagines himself burying his face in Nashkidil's silky hair, devouring her neck, tasting her plump lips, wondering if her secret flower is flavoured with orange blossom and rose too. The spell contained in the macarons brought him to the edge of an unbearable desire. Nashkidil is staring at him, charmed by his charisma.

He can see the surrender in her eyes; he is fascinated by their emerald sparkle, her golden hair, the soft contours of her angelic face, the beating of her chest calling for him. He has to have her! She is picturing him pulling the string attaching her robe, exposing her firm breasts, her exquisite skin, her graceful waist, her inviting hips.

She can't believe how warm and agile his tongue is. She has forgotten the feeling of letting go and giving herself entirely to a man. Only he, can make this natural, shameless and loving.

What a sense of victory when he penetrates her. They are one. Sensing his warmth, his vigour inside of her makes her feel alive, powerful, vulnerable and desired, her whole body is dominated by his virility. His large hands caressing her and holding her with force, in a gasp of ecstasy, she stops, looks into his eyes.

"I love you."

His expression becomes softer, and he whispers, "I love you too."

She can then let the wave of pleasure explode through her body, her nails digging into his back in an attempt to seize the moment, grip just a few seconds of ultimate felicity…no thoughts, no plot, no plans, she is just present, enjoying the two of them being just one — they are them, they are the universe. She moves on top of him and leads him to heaven's gate, slowly, his palms grabbing her voluptuous hips, she is moving deeply, in a hypnotic rhythm, rejoicing in the sight of him giving up control, again a thrilling sensation is growing in her loins, her being opening itself to the gift of a second orgasm. Now he can stop holding back and finally allow himself to climax, his semen filling her with a joyful delectation.

The last bit of ganache finishes melting in their mouths, and their gazes meet as if they are reading each other's thoughts. He's pulling the string of her robe; the luscious fantasy inspired by the enchanted macarons is about to become reality.

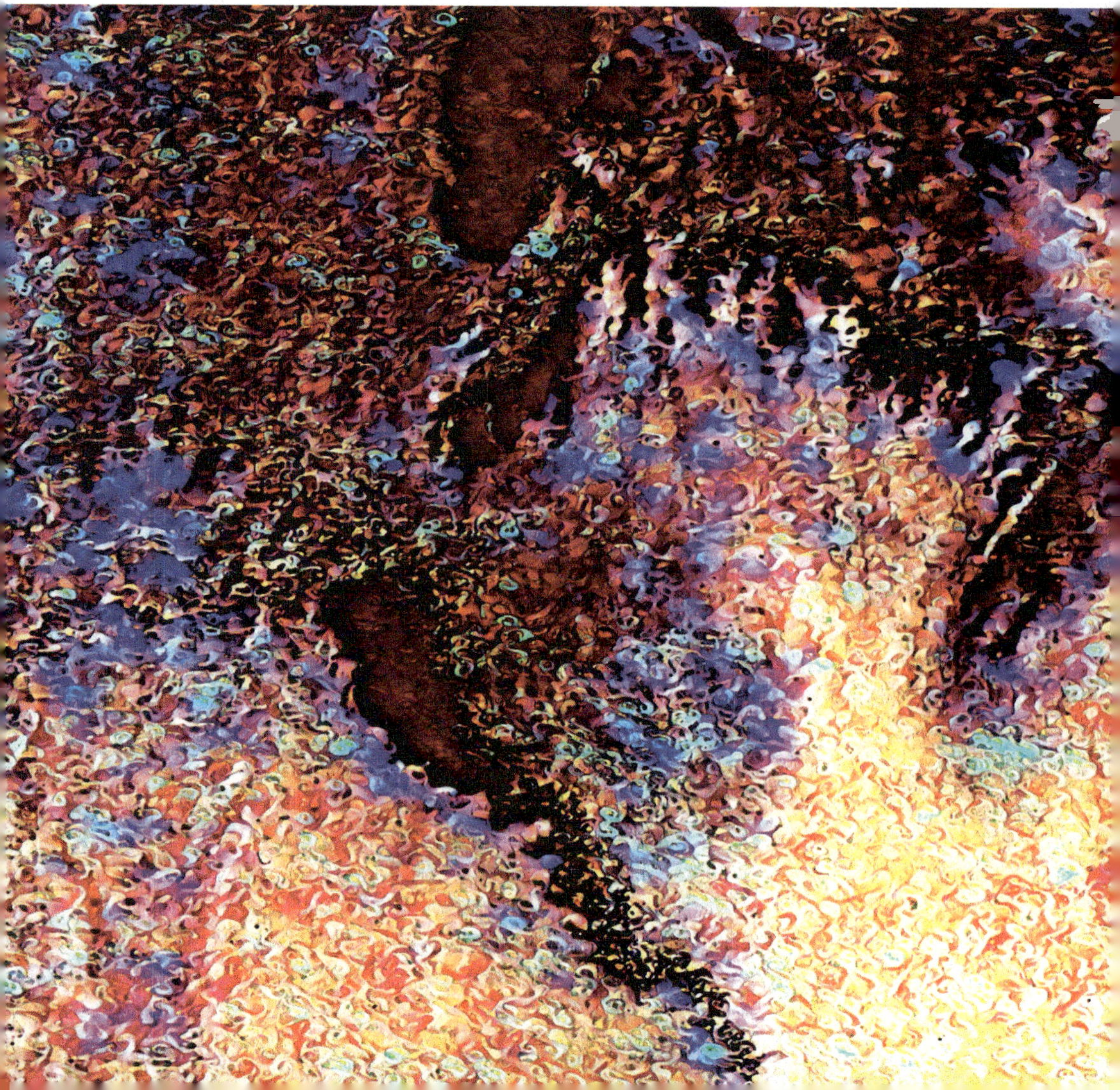

Oblivion

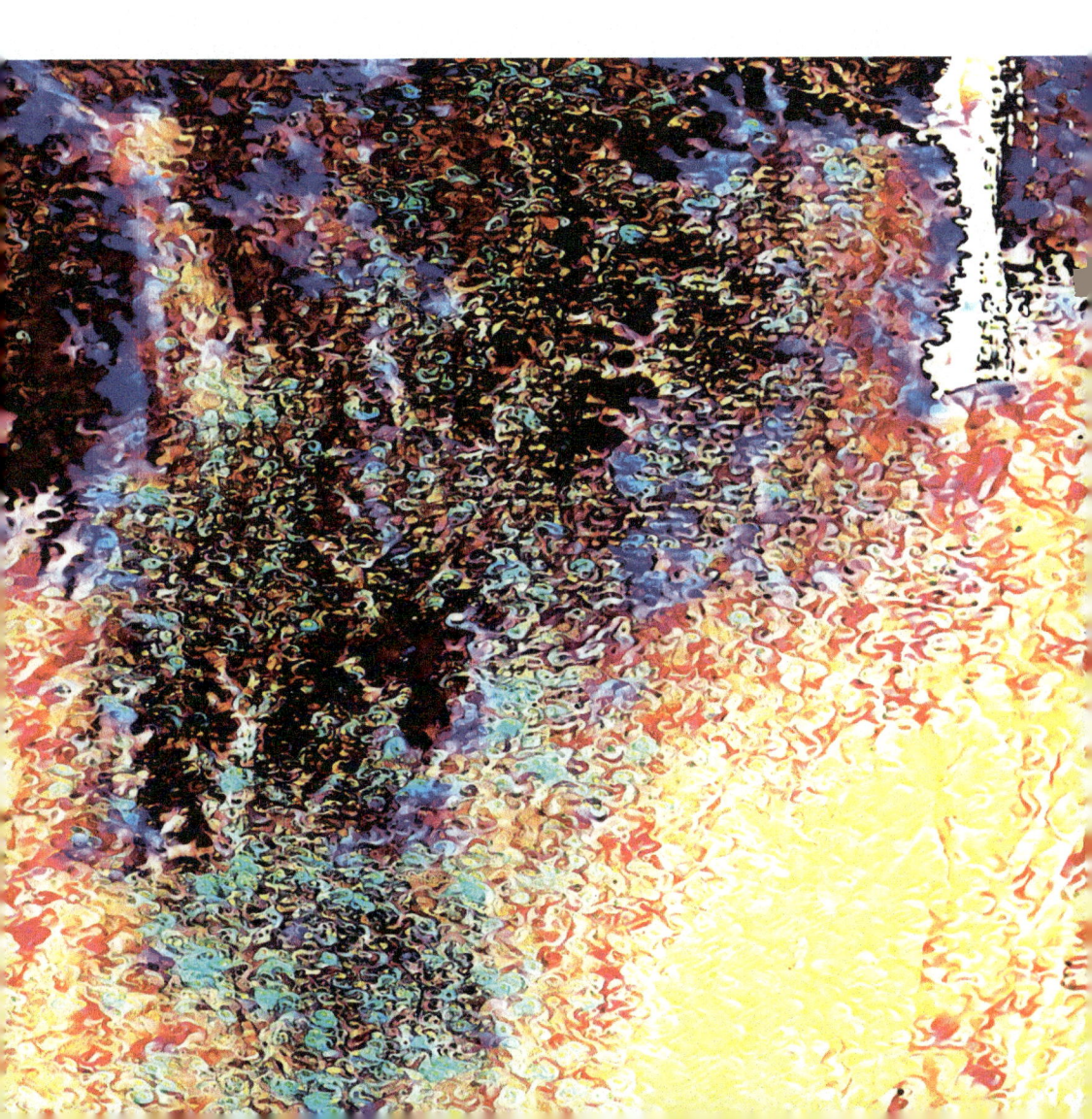

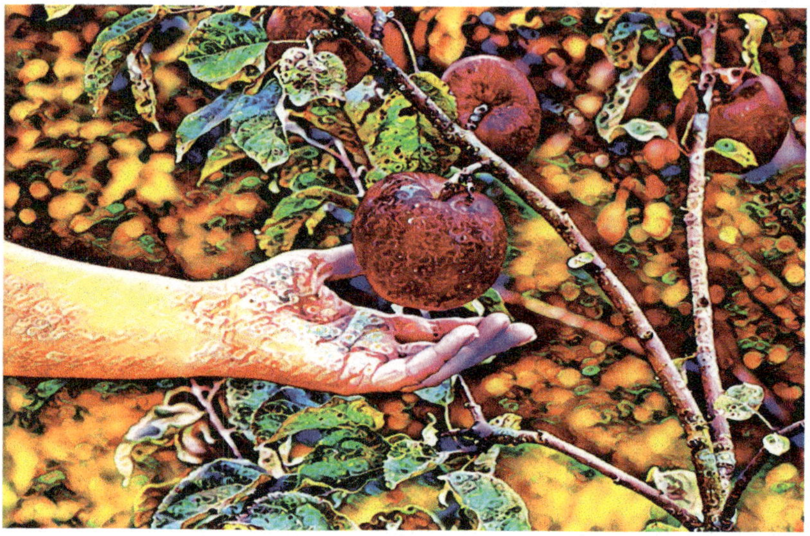

Guilt

Is a moment of pure intense happiness worth a lifetime of sorrow?

I am not to be forgiven; my torturer became my victim in an instant. Shame is eating my soul and I have to face my darkness and my weakness. But there was too much pain, too much to bear. I numbed myself, or I thought I did, when in fact I became even more cruel towards myself and instead of protecting the innocent girl I was, I killed her slowly…

I watched her tears, her struggle, but I strangled her anyway, reducing her resistance to silence. I blew out her light, smothering her in the limbs of eternal obscurity.

Guilt is a funny little thing, popping in at any time, sticking with me like chewing gum on a shoe when I thought I locked it in a box and threw the key away, fighting any coping mechanism I put in place. Its eagerness has no limits, feeding itself from forgotten memories, seizing and ripping off a lifetime of virtuous conduct.

There was nothing to save any more, nothing to be dignified any about more. That was the second when I became ordinary.

She Devil

You may not be aware of it, but you are surrounded by demons of the vilest species. You certainly have one in your closest circle, amongst your family and relatives, your friends or co-workers. Most of the time, you don't notice her. Yes, this evil is a she, a succubus sucking life away from you. Behind her innocent look, she has no morals nor values whatsoever, when it comes to the elixir of life. She is insatiable, stealing from toddlers to grannies, from the executive woman in her thirties to the blind widow in her eighties, taking from them their most precious treasure, the only thing on earth giving them unconditional felicity and vitality. Without shame nor remorse, she looks at them dying slowly, enjoying seeing their intense emotional and physical pain, savouring her victory with a cold hearted grin.

Who is she? She is seductive and dangerous, hidden behind the angelic smile of a child or the caring nature of your own mother or daughter. Once possessed, there is no way back, their innocence is lost forever. She is imperceptible, unseizable, mastering the art of deception, lurking in your home or in your office day and night, charming you with sweet words and virtuous behaviour, hypnotising you behind her irreproachable outward appearance. She may go to church every week, volunteer for the ones in need, she may be an honest wife and mother. Don't be fooled by her satanic abilities to blend in. All of this is a lie. She will carefully plot, cheat and even threaten to get what she wants from you when she's starving.

However, she may expose her malicious nature when satisfied, once she has won. Too proud to hide her infamy, she shows off her trophy in order to reveal her power to make your existence miserable. And she will do it, all over again, when she has a chance. You can hide your paragon anywhere, she will find it as sure as a dog finds a bone buried in a field. She is your worst nightmare. She is the Chocolate Thief.

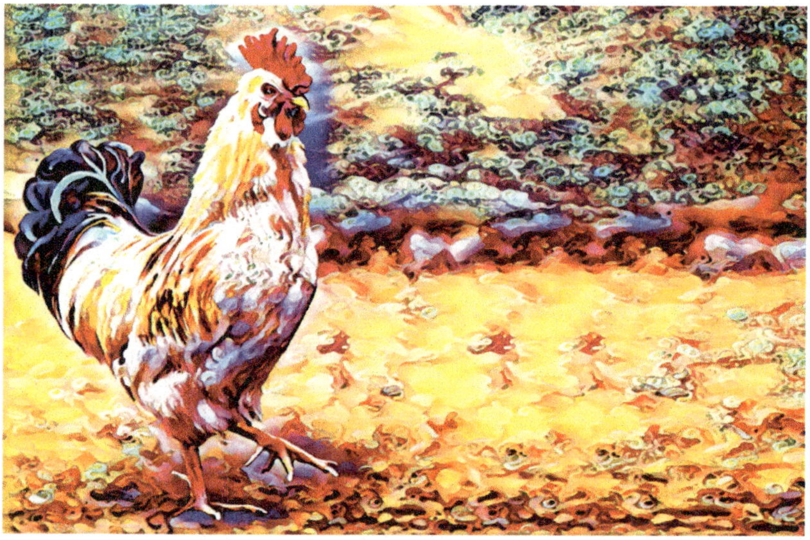

The Devil's Chicken

Knife in hand, I went to see if I could catch that chicken. The one that always avoided laying eggs, the one with the red evil eyes, the one responsible for the scars on my ankles, the very one that filled my nights with terror. I have always been reluctant to kill animals, since, as a city child on summer holidays at a friend's grandparents' farm, I saw a duck being decapitated in front of me, its beheaded body running around in a desperate attempt to live despite the lethal amputation. I was five years old, speechless in the face of this inexplicable bloodbath.

This morning though I decided to slaughter the wicked white-feathered beast — not to cook a nice Sunday roast, as I was afraid its flesh would corrupt us, infiltrating our veins with its malicious traits and turning my family members into vile creatures. Still, it had to die, and quickly. I couldn't live any more with that shadow obscuring every aspect of my existence.

Ever since I rescued that apparently inoffensive chick, my life had become a disaster. My friends stopped visiting me, and every time I was meant to go out something happened: a leak, actually three in two weeks, leaving the house flooded with expensive repairs needed; my job interviews were postponed then cancelled for obscure reasons; and my boyfriend broke a leg on my verandah steps as he was coming to pick me up for a romantic date. I never saw him again.

Let's face it! For everyone, I was now bad luck personified, the worst part being that I didn't feel safe in my own house, the biped witch always observing me, its piercing eyes giving me the chill, silently menacing me. What have I done to deserve that?

Sleepless, jobless, penniless…I reached the point when I didn't want to find out any more; I just wanted it to stop!

The table was dressed, a nice white lace tablecloth inherited from my great-grandmother, the silverware from my grandmother, the crystal glasses gathered in a second-hand market nearby. It looked beautiful, immaculate, sophisticated: in one word, it was perfect. The roast beef and the vegetables were gently cooking in the oven, and the cake was ready — a chocolate one, for my twenty-fifth birthday, the candles sitting on the bench. The Champagne was chilling in the fridge, too. Everything was ready to host family I hadn't had seen in such a long time, but the devil was still walking free in my yard.

I took the biggest knife from my kitchen drawer and sharpened it consciously, slowly, every motion being a promise of a better life, a brighter future. It was a beautiful day, hot for early spring, flowers had already blossomed, and I could already see emerging tiny fruits from my citrus trees. I looked at the sky, so blue, no clouds — no, just one, in the shape of a chicken, mocking me.

The beast didn't run: it came to me, asking for a pat. I caressed its head before grabbing its neck and cutting its throat in a delicate but firm movement, holding its body against me in a loving hug, absorbing its last heartbeat. Guilt crushing me, I fainted.

ELDERLY WOMAN DIES

A ninety-five-year-old woman has been found in her yard by a neighbour on her birthday, having bled to death after sustaining a serious throat injury.

It appears to be a suicide. She had no remaining family, having lost many relatives during WWII, and not having married since. Although the dining room was all set for a family celebration, nobody can say who she was expecting. A white hen was her only company. It is now available for a good home; otherwise it will be sent to the pound.

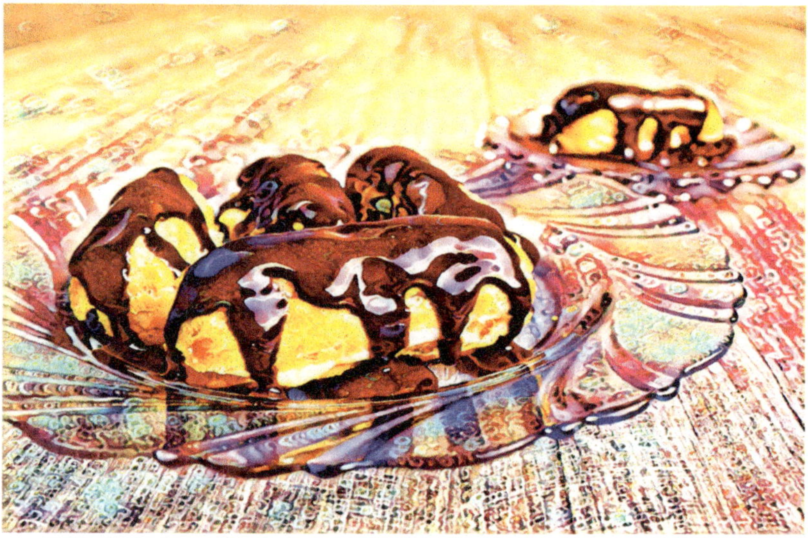

Find What You Love...

Find what you love and let it kill you
— CHARLES BUKOWSKI

There were many things that she loved that indeed could kill her. The only thing she had to do was choose her weapon for an exquisite death. Leaving this world enjoying the taste of what she had been forbidden to eat was a far more attractive idea than using the ordinary pills and alcohol cocktail. She didn't want to think about the unbearable pain and distress she would go through, shortness of breath, her throat closing, during the anaphylaxis such ingredients would trigger, nor the fact that she would need a very strong will not to use the Epipen in a last burst of her survival instinct.

She was already drooling at the thought of having Crème Chantilly with strawberries — why not have a fraisier, a French sponge cake she couldn't have for her birthday as a child, not that she was allergic to all dairy products already, but just because she was born in autumn, and there were no fresh strawberries at this time of the year. Her head spun with the endless possibilities of how she could use cream in her deliberate attempt to leave her dull life. Waffles, drizzled with rich chocolate sauce, topped with fresh strawberries or slices of bananas; or topping a rich decadent liégeois chocolate with ice cream, or just a warm viennois chocolate. What about a delicious crème pâtissière, flavoured with vanilla rum, in a strawberry tart or her famous éclair? Or just a simple flan parisien. Snickers ice cream? Possibilities, recipes filled her imagination with dessert tables, pictures of what she could have…and regrets for what she couldn't. There was no way she could enjoy all of them at once, she would be dead after the first one, so which to choose? What a dilemma! What would be the perfect combination of all she had missed over the last twenty years? And then came the how, and when. She wanted to leave this world in an ecstatic state, even if it meant an extremely painful death, so the pleasure had to be greater than everything she could imagine.

Her plan had to be perfect, not just a quick binging on something she craved for so long. It had to be agreeable to the eye and to the other senses. It had to be slow like a dance. She wanted to be won over by lust, desire and anticipation. She wanted her foreplay, as if she were making love for the last time and she didn't want it to end. End, ending, why the hell should there be an end to everything? Couldn't she just stop time and let herself float in a dimension of eternal felicity? She imagined the ideal setting, the flowers on the table, the delicately chiselled cutlery, the china plate, but she still couldn't picture which dessert she would choose as poison. While wondering about her passage to the afterlife, she enjoyed one of her lemon tarts: delicious, acidic, tingly, sweet enough, a little bite of happiness. She forgot for one minute all the frustration, everything she was missing, all the sorrow, the horrible feeling of not fitting in, not being normal. She forgot that she could die unexpectedly at any minute if a deadly ingredient sneaked into her meal. She forgot the need to take control of it, of her life, at every moment. For one minute she was happy. And that minute made her think:

today is not the day, let's think about it tomorrow.

Day after day, she postponed her suicide, losing herself in dreams of ultimate felicity, until the morning she finally made the decision. It was a beautiful day. Summer had finally arrived and the sun was warm enough for her to wear her favourite flowery dress. Paris' streets were crowded with tourists enjoying the sight of a picturesque fresh market, filled with delectable fruits, vegetables, spices and local specialities awakening their senses. She would celebrate her birthday early this year, because it was the last one, with a beautiful fraisier topped with a layer of pale pink marzipan, scattered with a few translucent delicate sugar roses. She stepped out of her apartment into the street to make her way to the luxurious pâtisserie of her district…too excited at the thought of the crème mousseline melting in her mouth, chunks of fresh strawberries flavouring it exquisitely…And as she rushed across the street that separated her from the pastry shop, absorbed in her reverie, a car hit her. Her head was crushed on the footpath. Her hand made a last attempt to reach the beautiful dessert in the window, in a desperate wish to survive few more minutes. Isabelle expired, the way she lived, frustrated, not being able to enjoy what she loved. Death had tricked her.

Blissful Lemon Tarts

PASTRY
(See petits sablés de noël recipe page 147)
Roll out the pastry until 3 millimetres thick.
Cut the pastry to the size of individual non-stick cases.
Line cases with pastry. Pierce the bottom with a fork and put back in the fridge for half an hour.
Then bake at 170-180 degrees Celsius for 10 to 12 minutes.
Remove from the tins and let the pastry cases cool down.

LEMON CURD
3 eggs
3 egg yolks
190 millilitres lemon juice
Zest of a large lemon
130 grams caster sugar
30 grams unsalted butter

Whisk lemon zest with caster sugar until it becomes a pale yellow scented powder.

Add eggs and egg yolks one by one while whisking.

Add lemon juice little by little still whisking.

Put the mixture over a bain-marie, and stir constantly with a wooden spoon until it starts to thicken to a creamy consistency.

Take off the heat and put the bowl over some cold water or ice cubes, to prevent it from cooking further and curdling.

Add butter, previously cut into dices and mix.

Wait for the temperature to cool down stirring all the time.

Pour the lemon curd onto the pastry cases, let it set.

The Heaven's Cook

I realise with shock that I've left the groceries on the bus…just as I am watching the taillights of the vehicle disappear round the bend. It vanishes under my stupefied eyes. Where did it go? How can I get back the trolley I've left behind the driver's seat? I am standing there, perplexed, disappointed and angry at not having the ingredients for tonight's celebration. The bus didn't turn at the corner, but just disintegrated into thin air, becoming gradually invisible. I shake my head, trying to make sense of what I just saw or didn't see actually, trying to reconnect my eyes to my brain. An optical illusion — that must be it! This white wine I had for lunch must have been stronger than I thought and I must be a bit tipsy, otherwise I wouldn't have blanked out like that.

Anyway, what am I going to do now? My employers are throwing this huge party tonight and I don't have the ingredients I need most. The next bus is in an hour and by the time I get to the small town the fresh market will be closed, and of course I have no phone coverage. You got to love the countryside! Going back to the domain empty handed, with neither the food nor the money my clients gave me — great impression! Well done for my first big job as a chef. I have no other solution than walking back to the mansion and pulling something together. I mentally go through all the recipes that might do the trick, combining products from the pantry, supplied daily by the domain's farm. They've just received a huge jar of fresh goat's cheese, and I am pretty sure there's cured meat in the cellar. What about goat's cheese mixed with chives and rolled in bresaola as an entree? Or a goat's cheese tart? Or a friand — a beautiful flaky, buttery puff pastry filled with goat's cheese, basil and a drizzle of olive oil? Olives! Why didn't I think earlier about that? There are so many olive jars on the shelves that nobody ever thought of opening. An olive cake, yum! That's what I am going to bake, and serve cold with a beautiful fresh and crispy garden salad. For mains, a vegetable lasagna. My throat tightens as I remember that all the vegetables I bought this morning are on their way to an unknown destination. Sweat runs down my back and I start shivering, as I am almost arrived. I start trembling, everything becomes fuzzy, I lose balance and as I am falling backward I grab a branch. But it's not hard — my hand is swallowed by something soft, and liquid starts running down my arm. I open my eyes, look at my hand…a tomato! A big round red juicy tomato! I am surrounded by an abundance of fruits, pink, red, orange, green, purple, yellow. I could swear they were not here two minutes ago, before I fell. What's happening to me? Where am I? The trees are overflowing on the path, so why not take advantage of the situation and harvest some, not many, just enough to save me from a disastrous mishap? Nobody seems to care about harvesting them anyway, so soon this profusion of fruits will go to waste or feed the birds. I jump over the little fence to pick apricots, peaches, cherries and plums when I see a wooden sign pointing to a tiny greenhouse: "More that way". I look around. Nobody on my left, nobody on my right, nobody behind. I am alone. Good! I run and sneak into the greenhouse, carefully opening the door to avoid any noise. It's bigger than it looks, and crowded with zucchini, eggplant and tomato trees. I gather some and place them in a basket I find near the door. It is so peaceful and beautiful in here, and a cool breeze is brushing my hair. Tiny drops of cold water splash my face; I can hear the water running and finally see a stream. I just want to sit here, cool down and relax for the rest of the afternoon. My eyelids are getting heavier. No! I can't fall asleep. It's time to go back and cook for tonight's party. I collect the basket, very heavy now, because it's filled with all I could find, walk back to the street, and almost run for the last kilometre to the domain. I rush into the kitchen, pour my findings onto the massive table, grab everything I can from the pantry and start cooking.

My hands are shaking as I place the last dish on the banquet table. It's extraordinary. I managed to prepare an entire feast in five hours. Now I can breathe. Someone grabs my arm.

"Wait!"

I turn back to see a gigantic man, maybe in his sixties, elegant and quite attractive.

"Julia, could you tell me where you bought the produce you used for this magnificent meal?"

"They all come from the area, sir — mostly from our hosts' farm."

"But why don't I see any roast or fish?"

"Today was so hot that they didn't keep well at the market," my cheeks are burning, and I look down as I continue, "so I preferred not to risk making anyone sick."

"Julia, stop lying please!"

The floor opens under my feet and I keep on falling. It's so bright my eyes hurt. I gasp — my stomach is going up my throat. Pins and needles all around my limbs, then nothing.

"I said, stop lying and be humble in front of your judge!"

What the hell is going on here? Who does this arrogant prick think he is?

He continues: "Do you really think a bus would vanish in front of you? We're not in a Harry Potter book: this is real life. Real death actually." And he starts laughing at his joke. "Now, allow me to introduce myself. I am Peter, Saint Peter." And he keeps on giggling. Great — I am dead, and my destiny is in a clown's hands. Any other bad news maybe?

"You have quite a record here: small lies, white lies, and you never repented. You stole some fruit from your neighbours when you were four, never confessed, didn't go to mass and history just repeated itself when today you decided to lie and steal again."

"It doesn't count!" I shout. "I was already dead! By the way, how did I die?"

"We'll talk about that later. Now I have to decide where to send you: Heaven is out of the question, so the options are Purgatory or Hell. As they say, the road to Hell is paved with good intentions, and you demonstrated that today."

I stand there, mouth open, speechless and in shock.

After this short but harsh sermon, Saint Peter grabs a piece of the olive cake and swallows it. He's about to carry on with his eternal speech about Good and Bad, when he stops. He takes a second piece of the olive cake, and this time he takes his time to savour the incredibly moist crumb, the subtle cheese flavour, the little pieces of ham and the olives, black and green. Double standards is all I can think about. He wants to send me to Hell for few little lies and he's obviously a glutton. Should I remind him that gluttony is a sin? He's just swallowing the entire feast while I wait for my sentence. Stop overindulging on my food! I have other things to do! Actually, now I have eternity in front of me, but come on! And he eats and tastes everything I prepared: the goat's cheese and bresaola rolls, the goat's cheese tart, the friand, the stuffed zucchini flowers, the eggplant lasagna, the strawberry tart, the peach tart, the apricot clafoutis, and he doesn't even explode. And I am starving. His eyes sparkles with sinful pleasure;

like a little child he licks his fingers and caresses his growing belly. What a ridiculous sight! I bite my tongue not to laugh. Saint Peter catches my gaze and tries to regain a certain composure, though he's just finished the very last bite of food on the table.

"I must admit that that was the best meal I have had in a very long time", he says, "and God knows I love my food." Yeah, tell me about it. "I have a peculiar offer for you. Our cook in Heaven is not as talented as you are. You wouldn't believe how many chefs, cooks and pastry chefs I have to send to Satan every day. Most of them are bad tempered, arrogant, narcissists and on top of that addicted to pretty much everything: alcohol, drugs, etc…It is literally Hell to find a good cook for us. Everyone thinks Heaven is Paradise — well not when it comes to food. You have sinned — lied, stolen a bit, but that's it. You're neither a drunk, nor a gambler, nor a cheater. You've got your pride, but a few centuries in my service will cure that. But most of all, your cuisine is what you would call on Earth a piece of Heaven. Do you want to work for me?"

Something is pinching my arm.

"Madame! Madame! Wake up! We've arrived, don't forget your trolley."

I open my eyes and look around; my head is killing me. I am still on the bus, alive, and very much in pain. Oh my God, that headache. I swear, I will not stop at the wine tasting before a big job ever again. I get off the bus and very carefully look at it turning at the corner to be sure it won't vanish.

The Painting

When Emilie was young and beautiful, she could eat whatever she wanted without putting on any weight. At the time, she was quite thin, almost skinny, although she could devour as much as a rugby team, and not the light healthy stuff. She used to eat rib eyes at four am after a long night of clubbing, lots of pasta, rice, cheeses, desserts and despite that abundance of heavy food, her figure remained quite athletic.

In her late thirties, Emilie was eating a bit less but started to put on few kilos, and then more, and more. She was desperate. Trendy diets, exercise, nothing worked. She finally reached that age when she realised that not only her beauty was fading: her health was suffering from her excess weight too. So she became self-conscious and vain, but most of all, she hated her body for having betrayed her.

There was a still life painting in her bedroom that she had inherited from a distant great aunt. It was very simple, very dark, very dry. One day, she looked at it, praying to not have to spend the rest of her life eating apples and pears in order to keep the rest of the figure she had. Emilie invoked the Universe to help her, God, Satan, pagan deities, whoever she could think of, even Dorian Gray's picture.

A few days passed, and miracle: she hadn't put on a single gram on her pretty strict and insipid diet. She contemplated the painting again, and maybe it was because of the spring's delicate sun, but it had become brighter, as if a spotlight were illuminating it. She didn't pay that much attention to it, but as the days got longer and sunnier, that picture seemed less and less depressing. She also started to indulge a little bit, as her weight was finally stable. Instead of consuming apples all day, she slowly switched to regular but healthy meals. Looking up at her bedroom wall, she realised that overnight new components had appeared in the painting — all those ingredients she added to her diet were there. Looking down her waist, she was astonished to see her clothes getting loose. She rushed to the bathroom, jumped on the scale. Yes! Three kilos! She had lost three kilos. Rejuvenated and happy that eating more might get her younger self's figure back, Emilie was hopeful and felt beautiful again.

Weeks passed and she was gorging on decadent desserts, full of chocolate and cream, stuffing her mouth day and night. She had eventually recovered her twenty-year-old body, and life was in front of her. The painting was getting busier by the day — it now looked like a bacchanalian banquet. Fruits and desserts of all sorts were overflowing from the table, even from the frame itself, exhaling enchanting aromas as soon as she entered the room. She just had to grab everything she wanted from the painting and eat it. Her bedroom became a realm of pleasure of all senses, satisfying all her gastronomic fantasies. She didn't need to go anywhere else. That was her happy place. As all her desires were fulfilled, she invented more, dreamt about three-star restaurant menus, cocktail parties, cheese and wine degustations. All of it was available at her fingertips. It was Paradise in her small apartment.

Until that moment when she couldn't control her weight loss any more. Emilie had already lost several dress sizes and needed to eat more and more to keep some decent level of energy. She stopped all exercises but kept on becoming thinner and skinnier. Her hair was dull, her skin greyish and dry: she looked like a ghost. Over tired and sick of having to eat more and more to be able to put one foot in front of another, she realised she had signed a pact with the devil without knowing it. All she wanted was to stop this nonsense and stop eating all together. Feeding herself was torture. Everything tasted like cardboard now, no more delightful scent came from the painting, which was gloriously expanding on the wall. She couldn't stand the sight of it any more and put it in a closet with the hope that it would reduce its power. But no. She was slowly perishing, with just skin and bones left on her body.

Emilie's body was discovered few days later. Death by starvation. What a sight, a middle-aged woman's corpse, lying on her bed, surrounded by chewed walls and a piece of what looked like the remains of a canvas in her mouth.

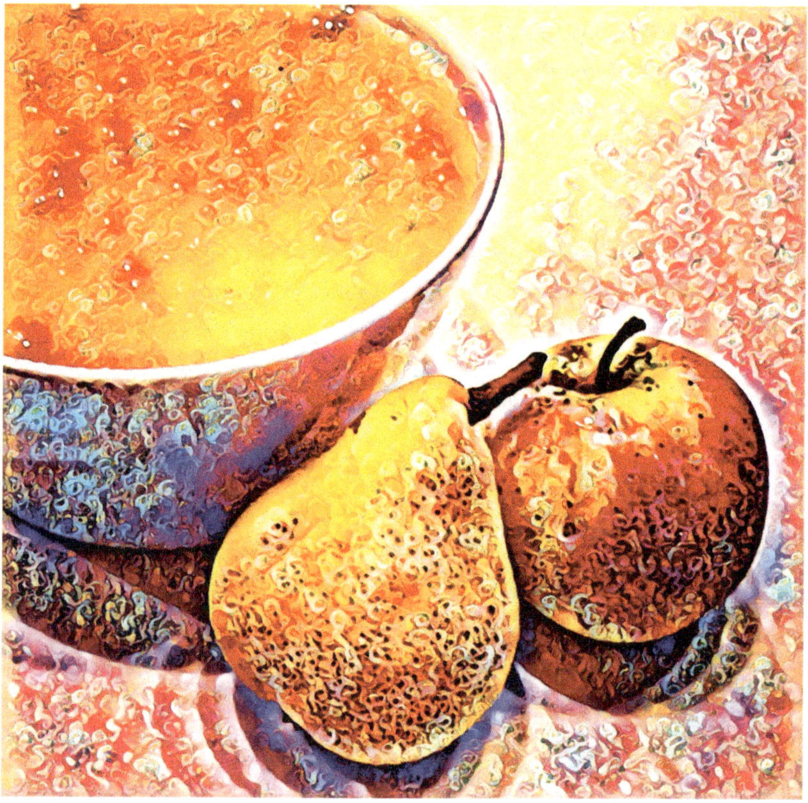

Apple-Pear Puree

The ratio is 2 pears for 4 apples.
2 pears
4 apples
Water
Raw sugar
Lemon juice

Wash the apples and pears then peel, core and cut them into quarters.

Drizzle them with lemon juice.

Place around 5 centimetres of water in the saucepan and add the fruit.

Bring the fruits to the boil, then gently simmer until soft.
Stir often.

Using a fork mash the fruits into a puree.

Add raw sugar to your taste. I use 1 teaspoon to 1 tablespoon.

It's ready. You can add some cinnamon right at the end, or throw a split vanilla bean in the saucepan at the beginning, depending on how you want to flavour the puree.

Infancy

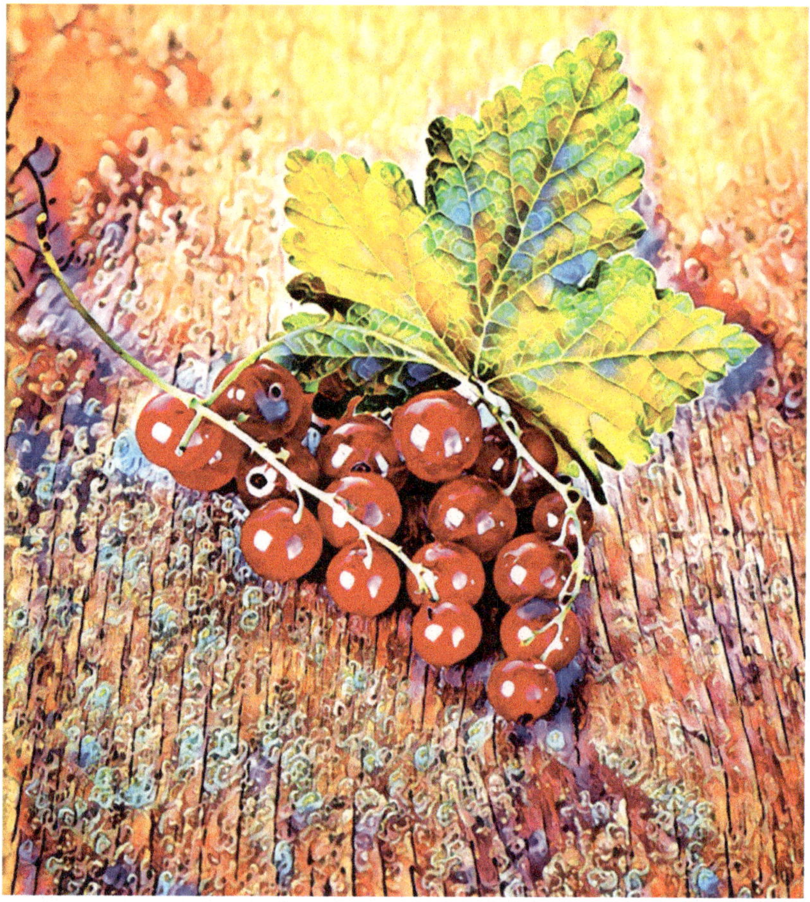

Berries

Have you ever tasted a wild berry? You know, gorged with sunshine, the one that fought against the elements to rise and fill.

Do you remember how it was? I am sure you do — not just the flavour, but the whole experience?

Berries are amazing little bites of goodness bringing us to heaven. It is an exhilarating feeling to pick them up undomesticated.

It was summertime in Tignes, a high-altitude ski station in the French Alps. I was on holidays with my daughter, who was eight years old at the time, and we used to go hiking: either together or her with the kids' club and me with the adults. That day we were on separate trails, as my trek was a bit difficult.

In a group of twenty, I was walking on a narrow path on the side of this beautiful bucolic mountain, alpine scenery at its best. After quite some time in the shade, we finally arrived on the sunny slope. It was warm and I was making the most of the beauty of nature around me when I spotted pink dots on the side of the track. I looked closer, and was amazed to find they were tiny wild raspberries. I was about to pick one when the guide told me not to because they could make me very sick because a fox may have peed on them. Well, that was the first time I'd seen those berries growing outside of a greenhouse, and

I hadn't known before they could grow at such high altitude. There was no way I would miss out on them.

While everybody was passing by me, I gathered many, threw them in my pockets and tasted one. They were much smaller than the ones you find in the shops, but they were so sweet, tasty and juicy…a real concentrate of flavours.

At the end of the day, I came back to the hotel room, picked up my baby girl and was very proud to show her my discovery. She too had gathered some berries during the day and kept them in her pants pockets. Like mother like daughter. She showed me beautiful red currants, little shiny red balls, still a bit acidic though, but we ate them all.

Last night I dreamt I was in front of a huge bush of blackberries and was about to grab one when I woke up. I then remembered the time my mum told me how dangerous it was to be around those bushes because they were full of snakes.

But I found a solution: I would go horse riding in the salt marsh and we would pick them up from the horse. I am not sure if it was less perilous but it felt like it. So imagine me, at the end of a hot summer's afternoon, stopping after a gallop, savouring those precious bites of deliciousness and then calmly finishing my ride towards the beach to watch the sunset. That feeling of freedom, enjoying the amazement of nature and its beauty, and that thrilling satisfaction of having eaten the forbidden fruit, is indescribable.

Year after year I went on those rides to savour the best blackberries I ever had. No others can compare to them, no others that you could buy in the shops have this sweetness and concentrated flavours given by the harsh condition of drought and strong sun.

Here in July it's winter, but in France it's summer. I am envious of all my friends enjoying our beautiful stone fruits such as Burlat cherries. Photos are all over my Facebook, with a variety of recipes such as clafoutis, pannacotta and other tarts. But what I miss the most are the apricots from the Guard region. Their roundness, their colour shading from apricot to reddish on the sides as if they had a bit of sunburn or if they are flashing with shyness. They are big, plump, incredibly juicy and sweet. They look like cheeky little bums, full of flavours, gorged with sun from the Midi; you can almost hear the cicada singing; you can almost taste the anise aperitif.

Just thinking about it I am drooling in front of my computer screen, thinking of recipes I could make with apricots, anise and almonds: a tart, a clafoutis, those homemade desserts which are so comforting, so summery and so regressive.

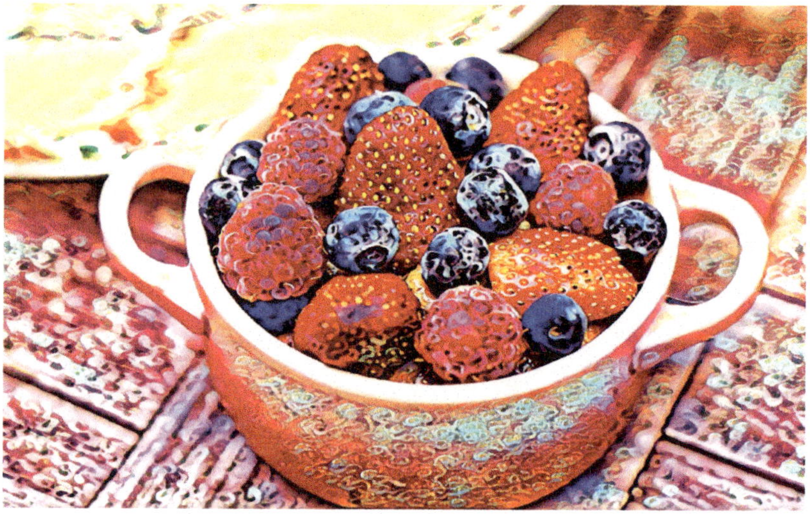

Sweet Berries

1 punnet strawberries
1 big juicy lemon
2 tablespoons vanilla sugar
½ punnet raspberries
½ punnet blackberries

Gently wash the fruit under cool water, pat them delicately with a soft cloth. Keep the blackberries and raspberries aside. Remove the leaves from the strawberries, and cut then in half (quarter if they're big).

Put the strawberries in a bowl and sprinkle them with vanilla sugar. Drizzle the lemon juice on top, stir well and wait for at least ten minutes.

Once the combination of those three ingredients has created a gorgeous syrup, add the raspberries and blackberries. Stir so all the fruits are deliciously sweetened, and enjoy.

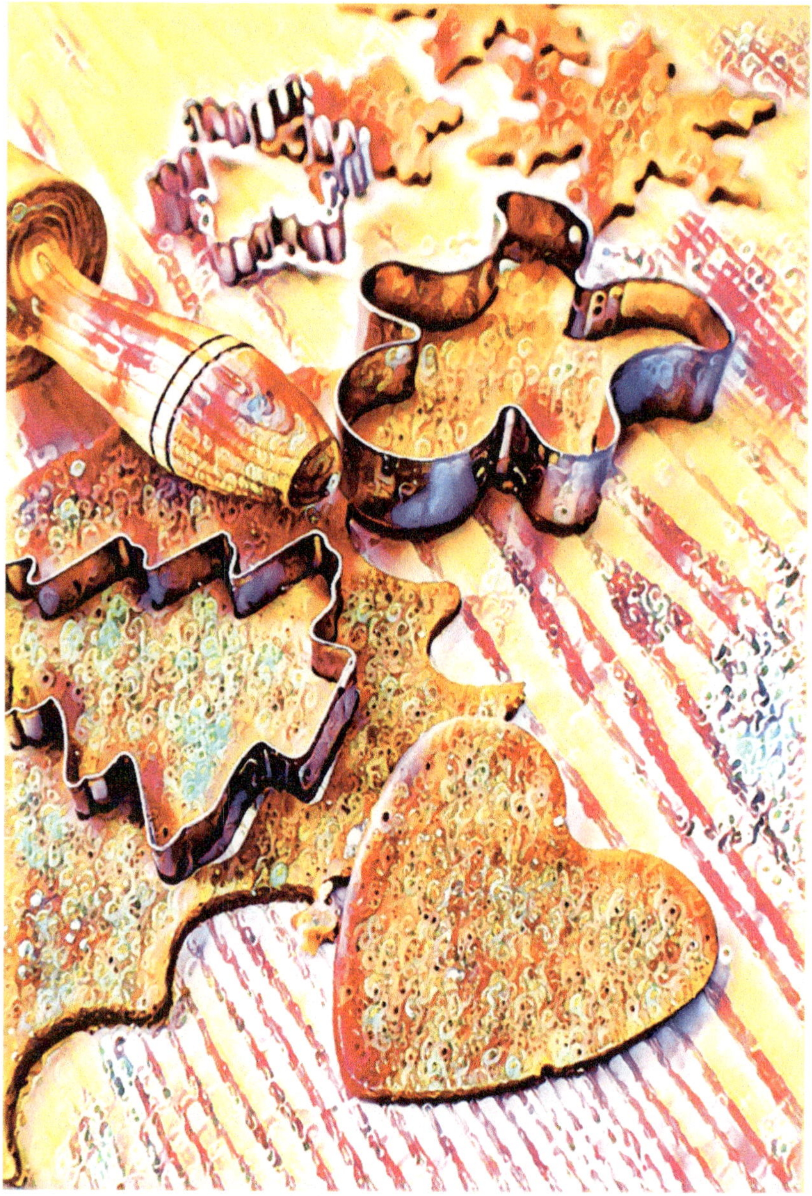

Christmas Shenanigans

There is a tradition at home I started when my daughter was a toddler. We make petits sablés de noël on the first day of December every year. It is the beginning of Christmas celebrations for us, to put us in the mood, because in France it's winter, cold, grey, depressing and the festive time helps us to fight gloominess. On the same day we decorate the tree, listen to and sing Christmassy songs.

I insist on the importance of children to "mettre la main a la pâte" — to put their hand in the dough literally — but which means to help. You take a very large bowl, and mix 275 grams of room-temperature unsalted butter and 200 grams of caster sugar until it becomes whitish. It is messy, it sticks to your hands but you are having a fantastic family time, aren't you? Then you add 400 grams of plain flour, and a small pinch of salt — now you understand why I specified a very large bowl! And you knead, then add 150 grams of almond meal. It gives a nice flavour to the biscuits and it's nourishing. Add two large eggs and a little bit of vanilla extract or even better, if you used vanilla beans before and kept them in a jar of sugar, add one to two tablespoons of this beautiful spicy sugar. Keep kneading until it's just combined, not too much. Then try to form a ball out of it; it is still sticky, well there is lots of beautiful butter in this recipe and you will thank me later. Put the ball on cling wrap and flatten it down so it will be easier to use after. Wrap it and put it to rest in the fridge for around three hours. It gives you all the time to clean up the kitchen, mop the floor and even to get the kids to have a nap.

After three hours, preheat your oven to 180 degrees Celsius.

Take the pastry dough out of the fridge, cut one third of it and knead it a tiny bit, just to break it down. Then there are two methods: whether you sprinkle the bench with flour and the top of your pastry so it is not going to stick to the rolling pin nor the surface, or whether you put it between two sheets of baking paper, it is totally up to you.

Roll the pastry to around four millimetres of thickness, and let the kids cut it with plenty of different shapes of cutters. Put a baking sheet on the tray and dispose the biscuits not too close to each other.

Whisk 2 egg yolks with a pinch of salt to break them down in a small jug, and brush the biscuits with them.

Put them in the oven for ten to twelve minutes until they're beautifully golden. Then let them cool down a bit on a grid to avoid condensation getting into them. And enjoy!

This recipe makes plenty of biscuits, so you can keep them in a metal tin for two to four weeks, but they won't last more than two days because you and the kids will have eaten them all.

Merry Christmas!

Petits Sablés de Noël

400 grams flour
275 grams unsalted butter
200 grams caster sugar
2 large eggs (plus 2 yolks for brushing)
150 grams almond meal
1 tablespoon caster sugar
Vanilla extract

Cheeky Little Girl

It is seven am on a wintry Parisian morning, and I am just getting out of a hot shower after my workout at home. I am about to tell Clémence to come for breakfast when I spot her just out of our tiny kitchen. She greets me with her most innocent look. My gorgeous little two-and-half-year-old girl, with her sparkling eyes and her cheeky smile, a dimple on her right cheek and a look which tells me she has been naughty.

I ask her if she was just eating the chocolate truffles we made last night for our traditional Saint Nicholas celebration, flavoured with just a tiny bit of rum, not enough to do any harm to a child, but sufficient to make those little bites scrumptious. Staring at me straight into my eyes, with an air of candid surprise, she says no, she hasn't touched any of them. Why would I think that?

She was so impatient yesterday when I wrapped the mini apron around her waist. I started heating the cream with a dash of butter, and she was over excited when the chocolate started to melt at the contact with the warm liquid, then turned into a shiny luscious ganache while she was stirring with her wooden spoon. I added my secret ingredient, a lid of fruity Caribbean white rum, and put the bowl in the fridge for it to set. That was the easy part — the hardest one was to convince Clémence to go for her afternoon nap. I had to tell her that if she didn't sleep, there would be no magic and we wouldn't be able to make truffles out of the ganache. I am not sure she slept, but she did stay quiet. She rose ready to get her hands dirty. I poured some Dutch cacao powder in a soup plate on the right side of what was too small to be called a table, the set ganache on the left, and four teaspoons, two for each of us…and we started spooning the decadent chocolate treasure, rolling balls in our bare hands, then again in the cacao. If the truffle was badly formed or too small, she wouldn't allow it to get to the next stage. Of course, what a shame it would be to waste, and hop in her belly!

Now with her standing in front of me, all innocent-eyed, I remind her that I am her mum, that I know when she lies, that I can see everything even when I am not in the same room because I have the mums' superpower and vision. She reiterates with a negative answer, very confident in her deceiving skills, despite her very young age.

I tell her I do know that she has been sneaking in the fridge to indulge in chocolate in the early morning, and that I will get very upset if she carries on lying.

Clémence, a bit disappointed she couldn't trick me, asks how I could know.

I am trying to stop the laughter growing inside of me, looking at all the little handprints on the walls and half of her face covered with the luscious ganache, and say: "I just know."

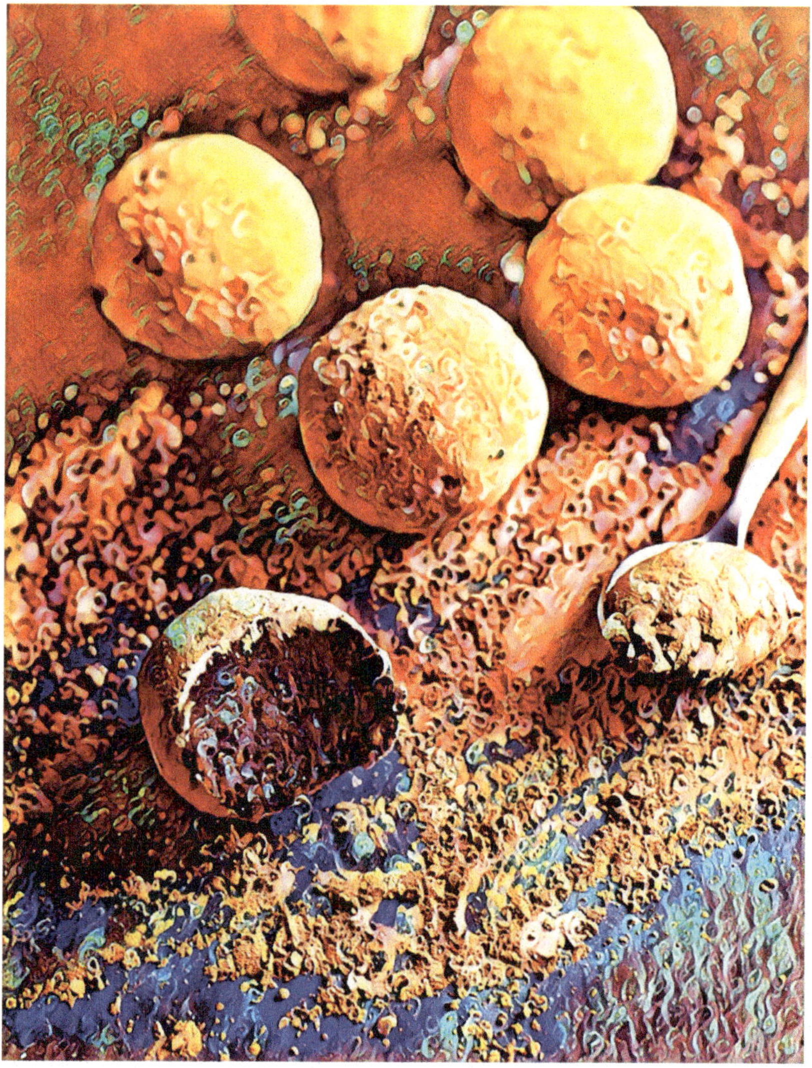

Chocolate Truffles

230 grams dark chocolate, at least 58 per cent
200 millilitres whipping cream
30 grams butter
1 lid vanilla rum
Dutch cacao

Clémence's Cake

I make the same movements for twenty-two years, repeating them year after year, without fail. It has to be done in secrecy. Late at night, when the house is asleep, I sidle into the kitchen. Tiptoeing around, as noiseless as I can be, I gather the ingredients. I arrange them on the bench in front of me, making sure I haven't forgotten anything. The recipe evolved over the first few years, making it more decadent, richer; but it is the same since nineteen years: 220 grams of dark chocolate (at least 58 per cent), 140 grams of caster sugar, 150 grams of butter, four eggs, 50 grams of plain flour and a pinch of fleur de sel.

    I switch the oven on at 150 degrees Celsius. While I heat the butter in a small saucepan, I put the chocolate to melt on a bain marie. I generously grease the round mould with some butter at room temperature. I put the caster sugar in a large bowl and pour the golden butter over it, and whisk with a fork until the mixture becomes whitish. Even though I am a pastry chef I don't use anything else for it. It is a ritual. It has to be done the same way as always. I then add the silky chocolate and mix until combined. It is now time to separate the eggs, mixing the orangeish yolks with the batter, setting aside the whites. I sprinkle the flour and make sure there are no lumps in my mix. At the second I switch the appliance on to whisk the whites and the pinch of salt, I have this sudden discharge of adrenaline: will she hear the noise? Nobody must know what I am doing. That's why sometimes I do all this before midnight and other times at five in the morning.

Now the whites are looking like snow, I delicately incorporate them into the mix, in three batches, bringing lightness to the batter. I fill the cake pan, and put it in the oven for 25 to 30 minutes, keeping an eye on it. I prepare one plate and a cake stand. Once the cake is ready I let it set out of the oven for few minutes, then put the plate on it and slip it upside down to take it out of the pan. And I flip it again with the cake stand. I pick the candles on it, put a lighter next to it, do the washing up and go back to bed, setting my alarm on.

I can't sleep; my mind is boiling. Anxious, I live that night again, every single minute of it: the fear, the pain, the unknown, then the excruciating joy, the tears of happiness, the relief.

I get up, exhausted, run back to the kitchen and light the candles, look at my watch, it's 6.10 am: the exact time she was born. I enter my daughter's bedroom, singing "Joyeux Anniversaire", carrying the cake, celebrating her arrival in the world and also taking a little bit of a revenge over the numberless nights she didn't let me sleep. Waking her up with her favourite cake and birthday gifts has become a tradition — it doesn't seem to her like a birthday if there is another cake instead, fancier, finer, decorated or not. This must be her cake and by extension our family birthday cake. Only people we care about and love very much are lucky enough to get it for their birthday. It is our silent way to say they are family.

Chocolate Cake

220 grams dark chocolate, at least 58 per cent
140 grams caster sugar
150 grams butter
4 large eggs
Pinch of salt
50 grams flour (optional)

If you want a gluten free/nut free version, just remove the flour from the recipe, it's to die for. Check in the oven more often as the baking time may be a bit different.

The Bet

"I will last longer than you!" Clémence dared me.

Which one of us will have enough will not to surrender to temptation? We were each opinionated as a bull and our pride was on the table. But what a stupid bet it was. We were now miserable, starring at the dessert, which we swore we wouldn't touch before the other did.

The mind is strange: psychologically if you can get whatever you want, you're not that much attracted to it, but if it's forbidden, it becomes the most precious thing to own. We are torturing ourselves.

We were already drooling at the thought of the first bite, the sensation when it would touch our tongues, imagining the intense pleasure of its texture in our mouths. It was torture and soon it became unbearable, but neither of us would give up. We were too competitive for that, and God forbid that we would show our weakness, our lack of will, just for a piece of cake. The pain was real: I could feel it in my stomach, in my muscles, in my bones. We were engaged in a battle, not only against each other but within ourselves. Self-control had to win over the rest, over temptation, over senses, over gourmandise. After all, we're human beings, not animals. So it shouldn't be that hard to resist, especially when we are well fed. It was not as if we were starving.

Each of us tried different techniques to control our appetite. I was trying to meditate, to think about something else, telling myself this beautiful cake wasn't there teasing me, calling me, that it didn't exist. My closed eyelids were burning though, my brain knowing exactly what was on the table and willing me to see it, smell it, touch it, embrace it and devour it.

So we went on and on for what seemed to be hours. When I looked at my watch, only fifteen minutes had passed. Why was time so cruel to me? It felt like an eternity. Looking at my daughter, I tried to guess whether she was about to give up, but she was holding on like a pro despite her youth. Was she more stubborn than I was? Was she more driven than I was? I took a few deep breaths, trying to shut down my desire, but it didn't work: there was that invisible hand squeezing and twisting my stomach. I couldn't stand it any more. At the very moment I reached for the plate with a hesitating hand, I saw her arm stretching too. What a relief! We both cracked at the same moment! We burst into laughter, cutting the cake in half to share it.

That feeling when I finally tasted it — so much joy — it was even better than I imagined. That was a cake we used to eat all the time, but just the thought of not being able to have it made it extremely appealing.

Friendship

Although I had no idea what I was going to eat as I was blindfolded, I was quite excited. I was scared Bianca and Naomi would make a joke and serve me some disgusting improbable combination of flavours. It was all my fault. I was the one who was constantly bragging about my ability to detect, eyes closed, every single component of a dish even if it had a dozen ingredients or more. Tired of my constant bragging, my best friends decided to put me to the test. So there I was, sitting on a couch in Bianca's living room, listening to them chatting and giggling in the kitchen, and what began as mild apprehension soon became clear anxiety. I started sweating, and moved around on the couch to find a position where I would be at ease, one which would allow me to stand up quickly and run to the bathroom in case I had to spit something really unpleasant out, or worse, in case I might vomit. What the hell was I doing there? I started to find the wait cruel — the weather was beautiful outside and I just wanted to be done with it.

"Are we going to do this now? Are you waiting for me to grow roots?"

"Coming, coming! Don't be so impatient! Savour the wait, hi hi hi… you're going to be surprised." Bianca yelled back.

My honesty will kill me someday. I could hear them laughing as they approached. I stopped breathing.

"Are you ready?"

I nodded timidly.

"Open your mouth — wider! Come on!"

I reluctantly obeyed. I felt the coldness of the spoon touching my tongue and hesitated one second before closing my mouth on it. How surprising! It was delicious!

"OK!" I laughed, totally relieved. "It's definitely chocolate, and there is a bit of vanilla, a bit of tonka, almonds…I am not going to enumerate all the ingredients of the meringue nor those of the succès. So it's a feuille d'automne with a twist! Not much of a test, you all know it's one of my favourite cakes. I expected you to be mean."

"Why would we be mean to you, especially today?"

"Why today?"

I felt the blindfold being removed.

"Open your eyes!"

I slowly opened my eyes and there were two dozen of my friends in front of me, while my daughter Clémence was in the middle, holding a feuille d'automne cake with candles.

"Happy Birthday Maman!"

"But my birthday is not until next week."

"We know, but as you wanted a surprise birthday party for your fortieth birthday, we decided to do it early so you wouldn't have time to find out if we were planning something or not."

I was surprised, happy, though I also felt a bit stupid not having figured them out, but most of all I was ashamed. I felt ashamed I ever thought my friends would play a nasty joke on me, of having doubted their good feelings, that I thought they'd be mean in their choice of dish. Even if it hadn't been for the surprise, they would have challenged me with something pleasant and delicious to taste. I didn't deserve them.

I was humbled and promised myself that I would never

brag again; maybe I could detect every ingredient of a complex dish, but I hadn't been able until that moment to detect the only component which was important in our relationships: unconditional love.

Pungency

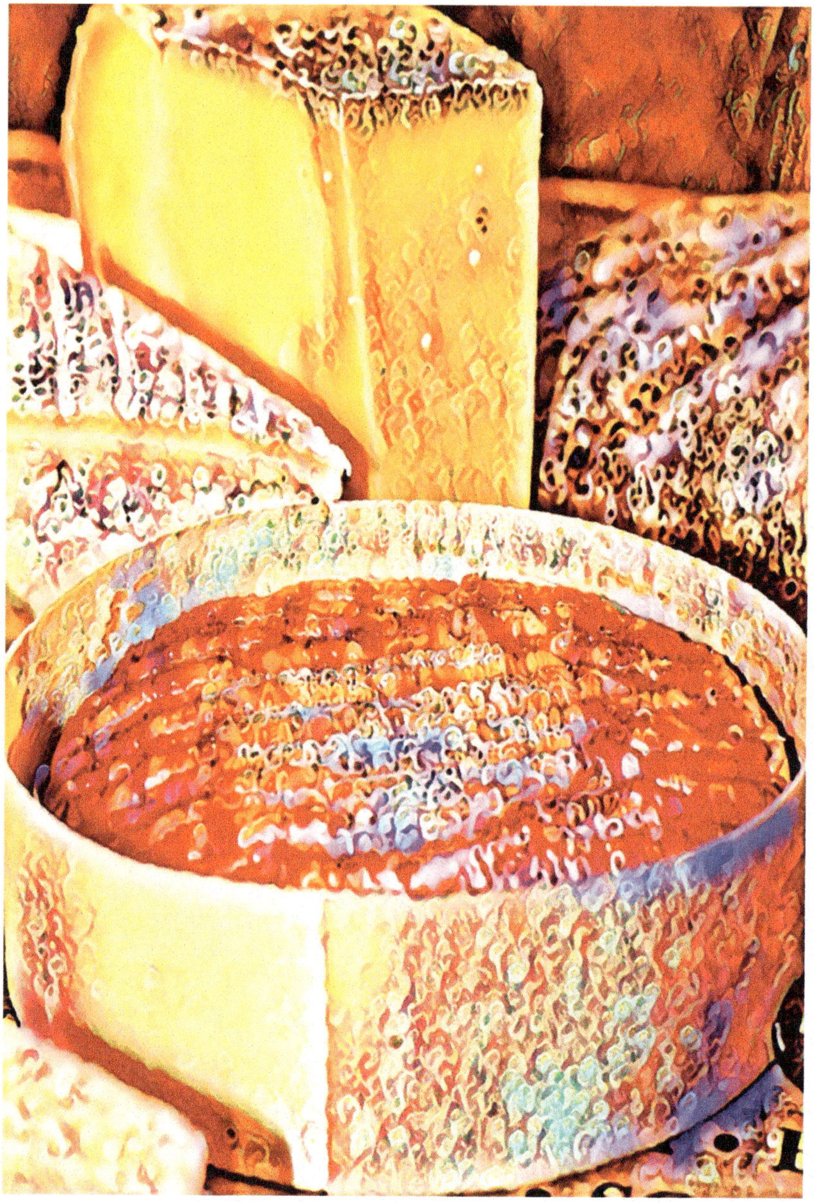

I Am an Addict

My name is Virginie, and I am an addict.

In my defence, I have extenuating circumstances. My parents have always been big users, since before I was even born. So I grew up surrounded by substances coming from various origins. My father would sneak even a little bit of that exhilarating drug in my mouth when I was a toddler.

During summer holidays, we had a morning ritual: we would drive to the island supplier and I would stay playing in the hippie farm's yard with the animals, while he would buy enough for the day. Then before going back to the house, just before lunch, he would give me my fix. My mother thought it was too much, but what could she do?

The substance was a big part of our lives; they would consume regularly and even more so when there was any kind of celebration. Birthdays, holy communions, weddings, Christmas and even Sunday lunches were an excuse to use even more, and get lost in the felicity procured by the still controversial substance.

Very early I learnt to recognise the quality, the provenance and became quite an expert. Later on, it didn't bother me to stride along Paris to gather the best product, although, year after year, good suppliers became almost non-existent. To me it was natural to use, even though many people were warning me about the dangers of it. I must confess, and not without shame, that unfortunately I passed this bad habit on to my daughter, and I am ashamed to admit it, but I even used with her, many times.

I thought we were saved when we arrived in Australia: the law being way stricter than France, it was harder for us to get our dose. As you can imagine, withdrawal was pretty tough on us. We went from angry phases to despair, urges twisting our guts, making us sick. But we had resources, even though we got pretty clean for several years. When the word came out that we could find what we needed we didn't spare any expenses to satisfy our sinful nature. We kept it exceptional though. After a traumatic ten-day cleanse, with rising anxiety, we couldn't resist any more and surrendered to our lowest urges. My daughter was begging me and my will disappeared.

So at five in the afternoon, I picked up my phone and rang a dealer. It took him thirty minutes to reach me. When he arrived, we were very excited. As soon as we closed the door on him, we looked inside the paper bag and discovered with joy the treasure we were waiting for. It wasn't the one we would have used in Paris, the best origin getting short in supply several months a year even there, but it was better than nothing. You do with what you have, right? With aroused pleasure due to anticipation, we unwrapped the Pont Levêque, the camembert, the brie and the goat's cheese, smelled them and placed them on a plate with rosemary crackers. Of course it would have been better if it had been with toasted walnut bread, topped with spring onions, and even heaven if it had been a runny raw milk Mont d'Or, which is impossible to source here; but this platter brought us so much happiness that I still can't describe with words how it felt when I ate it.

My name is Virginie, I am French, and I am a Cheese addict.

Risotto al Gorgonzola e Riesling

VEGETABLE STOCK
Water
1 carrot
1 large onion
1 leek
Salt

RISOTTO
1 large onion
1 bottle Riesling
6 handfuls arborio risotto
50 grams unsalted butter
50 grams grated parmigiano
125 to 200 grams gorgonzola

SERVE WITH
Mushrooms
2 slices bacon
Lemon juice

To make a delicious comforting risotto during winter: first prepare a vegetable stock. It doesn't take much time, and it's additive free. In a saucepan filled with water, throw an onion, a large carrot, the white part of a fat leek and a little bit of salt. Bring it to simmer, and leave it on the heat for at least half an hour.

Slice a large onion and cut it into cubes. Wet a large saucepan with white wine, just enough to cover the bottom. Don't use cheap wine; the better it is, the better the risotto will be. So pour yourself a glass of that delicious Riesling and sip it while cooking. Basically, the ratio is: one glass for the cook and the rest of the bottle will go into the risotto by the time it's ready.

Add around six handfuls of Arborio risotto, stir it in the wine so it becomes shiny. Lower the heat and add a ladle of vegetable stock, and repeat every time the liquid gets almost absorbed. Towards the end, add wine instead of the stock, until the rice is just cooked.

Remove from the heat, add a bit of unsalted butter and stir until all combined — this is called mantecare. Then add the grated parmigiano and at least 125 grams of gorgonzola, depending on your taste. I most of time keep going until almost 200 grams! Stir until it's totally melted.

In a saucepan, fry some sliced mushrooms with the diced bacon. Deglaze with the lemon juice.

Serve the risotto on a soup plate and top it with a spoon of mushrooms and bacon.

Pastoral Getaway

Raclette is a dish from the European Alps, originally from the Canton de Vaud in Switzerland. It is melted cheese that we eat with boiled potatoes, cured meats, cornichons and onions.

Many years ago, while we were on holidays in Villars sur Ollon, Clémence was around ten years old, we took a whole day hiking in the mountain with a guide. First we took the cremaillière, a cog railway, designed so it can go up during snowy months. This was in summer, but it's the only way to go up there. There was one stop before ours, near a restaurant, and goats were everywhere, naughty animals, jumping on tables and even trying to get on the train. Once arrived, we started our walk, which was beautiful — cows were walking free, no boundaries, no electric fences, each of them wearing a big Swiss bell. The mountain in summer is delightful, full of flowers, it is very picturesque.

We stopped after one and half hours to have lunch. The guide decided to prepare us raclette the way shepherds did it in the old days. She lit a fire, and found a slate to put next to it. She placed the cheese on the stone to melt. Meanwhile she slid a few pieces of bread to each of us. The cows were getting closer, crossing the path to come near us, as they were very curious about what was going on. The kids were playing around, and the adults were enjoying wine that had been previously chilled in the lake. In front of us, the mountain displayed all its magnificence, herds of chamois and ibexes were peacefully climbing the rocks. Once the cheese had melted enough, our guide scraped it over a piece of bread and gave it to us. That where the dish got its name: raclette basically means scraped cheese. While we were enjoying our lunch and the cheese was still melting on the slate, three cows came to check on the fire and on the cheese. We had to physically push them away so they wouldn't eat our sustenance. The herds of chamois were running down the mountain quite close to where we were, which is extremely rare as they are very shy and usually avoid being close to humans, but they felt confident enough as we were not noisy or moving near them.

Lunch done, we packed up, had a last look at the beauty and started to walk around the lake. Then we arrived at a little cottage, very bucolic with its potted flowers and farm animals running everywhere. The hostess showed us around, and challenged the kids to catch a chick. Clémence caught a hen straight away and was very proud of herself, and so happy to cuddle it. The hostess made us afternoon tea — a tray filled with homemade brioche and strawberry jam: it was fantastic. We headed back to the train a little bit before five, and stopped at the stable to have a look at the cows with their calves. The farmer taught us how to milk a cow with our bare hands but I was terrible at it — it took me five minutes to get few drops! Clémence was a natural though, and the milk was flowing for her. She drank it just warm out of the teat. For a city girl it was quite an achievement and a wonderful experience. Unfortunately her mood was soon darkened by the sight of a sick calf, and she was hurting so much for it. After that, she never wanted to eat veal ever again. She doesn't eat lamb either: no baby animals as they are too young to be mean. Yes, I am guilty of having told her that we only ate very mean adult animals when at three years old she decided it was cruel to eat meat.

We had a good laugh once we got back to the hotel, as we heard that one of the staff bedrooms had been totally messed up during the afternoon by a fox cub, which made its way via the window and was comfortably asleep in the middle of the bed when the room's occupant came back from work.

Ah Switzerland is such a beautiful country, where humans and wildlife are living well together.

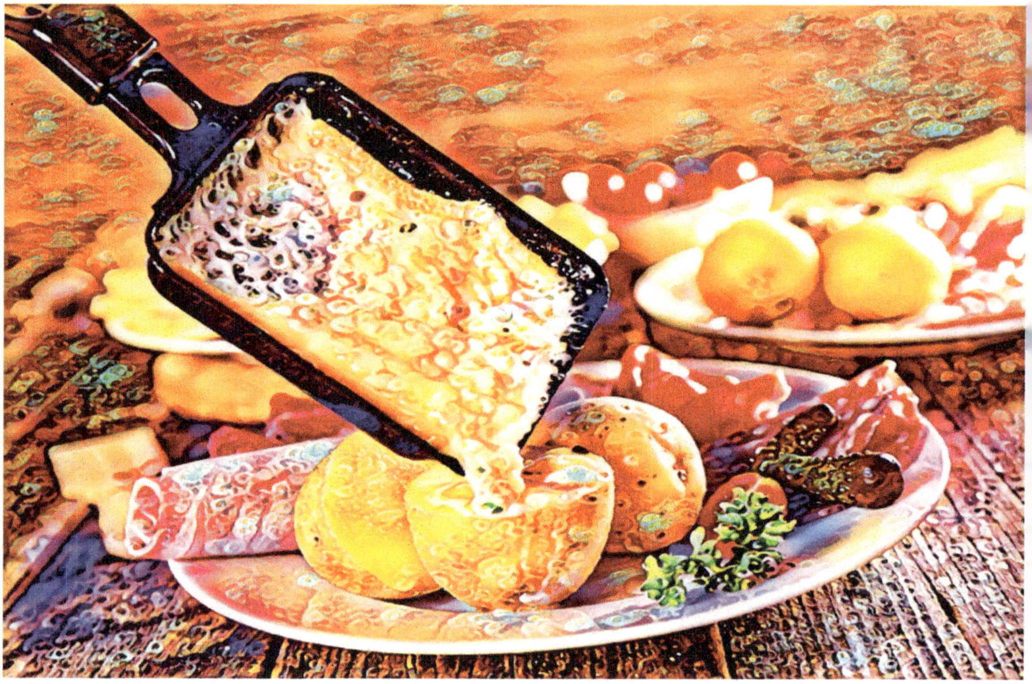

Raclette

400 grams raclette cheese
10 slices prosciutto
10 slices bresaola
5 slices ham off the bone
6 to 8 potatoes
3 large spring onions
Pickled onion
Gherkins (not the sweet ones)

If you have the chance to get a raclette machine, some cheese shops rent them, try this meal during a cold evening.

Boil the unpeeled potatoes.

Prepare a luscious plater with the cured meats and condiments.

Put your cheese under the grill.

Place a potato cut in half on your plate, with some cured meat and condiment.

Once your cheese is sizzling, let it slide on the top of the potato.

Eat it very hot, as it's better like that.

White wine is usually recommended to match this dish, as it will cut the fat and make it easier to digest.

About the Author

Parisian born and bred French pastry chef, V.P Colombo, currently lives in Sydney where she founded and ran *Fleur de Sel*, a homemade cake and dessert business, before dedicating her time to writing. Her macarons, like all her food created without artificial colourings and preservatives, were much loved at the Balmain market in Sydney, as were her scrumptious dessert tables created for weddings.

V.P left Paris, via Singapore, to arrive in Sydney in 2010, and stayed in Australia to create stability for her daughter. The challenges of immigration were compounded by severe depression and life threatening food allergies.

A Little Bite of Happiness emerged through this period as these challenges, combined with her passion for food, sparked her imagination as a writer. The resulting book, her first, is an homage to food, sensuality, love, loss and simply life in all its glory.

CPSIA information can be obtained
at www.ICGtesting.com
Printed in the USA
BVOW05s0452260917
495784BV00011B/39/P